Dressage Training
Customized

ALSO BY BRITTA SCHÖFFMANN

Klaus Balkenhol: The Man and His Training Methods

Dressage School: A Sourcebook of Movements and Tips Demonstrated by Olympian Isabell Werth

Britta Schöffmann

Dressage Training
Customized

Schooling the Horse as Best Suits His Individual Personality and Conformation

Translated by Lilliana Joseph

TRAFALGAR SQUARE
North Pomfret, Vermont

First published in 2010 by
Trafalgar Square Books
North Pomfret, Vermont 05053

Printed in China

Originally published in the German language as *Jedes Pferd ist anders* by Franckh-Kosmos Verlags-GmbH & Co. KG, Stuttgart

Disclaimer of Liability
The author and publisher shall have neither liability nor responsibility to any person or entity with respect to any loss or damage caused or alleged to be caused directly or indirectly by the information contained in this book. While the book is as accurate as the author can make it, there may be errors, omissions, and inaccuracies.

Library of Congress Cataloging-in-Publication Data

Schöffmann, Britta.
  Dressage training—customized: schooling the horse as best suits his individual personality and conformation / Britta Schöffmann.
    p. cm.
  Includes index.
  ISBN 978-1-57076-453-0
  1. Horses--Training. I. Title.
  SF287.S38 2010
  636.1'0835--dc22

                      2010000157

Photo credits: Alois Müller (pp. iii, vii, viii, ix top, x bottom, 9, 10, 11, 13, 14, 18, 24, 27, 34, 35, 36, 38, 39, 41, 46, 48, 50, 66, 79, 84, 85, 87, 89, 90, 91, 92, 93, 95 bottom, 97, 98, 99, 100, 101, 102, 103, 105, 109, 110, 111, 118, 120, 121, 122, 125, 138, 139, 146, 147, 149, 154, 155, 156, 157); Hugo M. Czerny (pp. x middle, 43); Jan Gyllensten (p. 71); Nina Kleinbongartz (p. 68); Lothar Lenz/Kosmos (p. 145); Hannelore Peter (pp. 94, 95 top); Julia Rau (pp. v top, xiv); Christof Salata/Kosmos (pp. 16 right, 73, 74, 107); Bärbel Schnell (pp. v middle and bottom, vi, ix bottom, x top, xi middle and bottom, xii, 5, 6, 7, 8, 22, 45, 53, 54, 61, 62, 76, 78, 81, 82, 88, 104, 119, 124, 132, 134, 137, 140, 142, 150, 151, 152, 153, 158, 159, 160, 161, 163); Britta Schöffmann (pp. 28, 69, 94, 95 top, 131); Edgar Schöpal/Kosmos (pp. 64, 66); Christiane Slawik/www.slawik.com (p. 83); Horst Streitferdt/Kosmos (pp. 1, 2, 4, 8, 15, 16 left, 17, 31, 59, 164); Jacques Toffi (pp. xi top, 21, 129); Julia Wentscher (p. 127)

Illustrations by Cornelia Koller

Many thanks to Doris and Karl Driehsen, Barbara Hansen, Franziska Jäger, Tanja Leipack, Christine Palmer, Inga Thielen, and Bärbel Schnell, who very kindly allowed themselves and their horses to be used as "models."

Book design by eStudio Calamar
Typefaces: Scala, Scala Sans

10 9 8 7 6 5 4 3 2 1

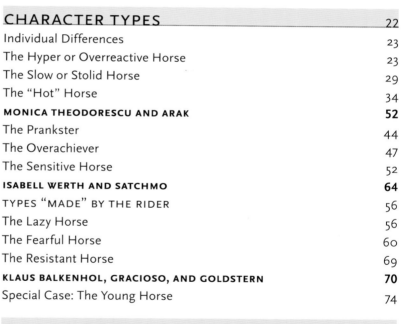

HORSES ARE INDIVIDUALS

How to train a horse according to his "type" (I discuss what constitutes "type" below) is a theme that I am confronted with daily and have long contemplated. Over the years I have been acquainted with the most interesting horses. They were each so different from one another, both to handle and to ride, and were individuals, just like you and I.

Obviously, some horses are big and powerful, while others are small and dainty. Many are calm or even stolid, while others are sensitive or nervous. Some are very clever while others are slower to comprehend. These differences, combined with breed and gender characteristics, help distinguish between *types* of horses. Character aside—a Friesian has particular strengths, while a Thoroughbred has others, and a mare will react to a situation in ways that a stallion or a gelding will not. These variations must be taken into account during daily handling and riding.

A very skilled rider can adjust appropriately to almost any type of horse. A less experienced rider should at least be able to identify his own horse's type and ride him accordingly. Regardless, the Training Scale (see p. 17) should provide a guiding principle for all riders, whether they practice dressage, jumping, eventing, or simply ride for pleasure. The Training

Even though Courbière (above) and La Picolina (p. viii) are similar in color and build, their characters are like fire and water, and they are completely different to ride.

Scale is not rigid and restricting (as ill-informed critics sometimes argue) but rather a thread that can be finely woven into an individually tailored training plan, allowing each horse to achieve his potential.

It is beyond the scope of this book to deliver an instruction manual for riding *all* horses. Riding is much too complex for that, and the characteristics of horses and riders are too varied. Rather, this book is intended to provide a practical guide, which—when combined with classical principles—can help those riders who would like to train their horse in accordance with his individual type, regardless of his level or quality or whether he is a trail horse or talented competitor. Above all else, riders must remember that when training horses, all cannot be trained in exactly the same way or pressed into the same mold.

BRITTA SCHÖFFMANN

WORDS OF WISDOM FROM TOP RIDERS

"It is immensely important to cater to a horse's individuality. In order to do this, one must have a command of what I call 'horse language.' This takes years to learn. The worst mistake a rider can make

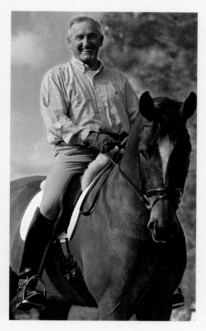

is to fail to discover and accept a horse's personality. By oversimplifying horses and lumping them all together the rider risks 'breaking' them and taking away their spark. Acknowledging the individuality of each horse must be a first priority for every rider and trainer."

KLAUS BALKENHOL
Olympic Medalist, World Equestrian Games Winner, European Champion, German Champion, World-Class Trainer, Former Chef d'Equipe of the US Dressage Team

"No two horses are the same. One must analyze each horse, considering his character, anatomy, and eccentricities. For each horse there is a 'key,' and it is our task to find it. There is no style that can be imposed upon every horse. Each must be individually evaluated and handled accordingly. This, however, cannot be done in half a year; the process takes a while to evolve. As a rider I must make myself aware of the dynamic development of a horse and adapt myself to it."

ISABELL WERTH
Olympic Medalist, World Equestrian Games Winner, European Champion, German Champion, World Cup Winner

"Each rider has his own signature style: an approach to working with the horses he rides. However, we must all be ready to alter our 'signature' according to the individual horse's needs."

NADINE CAPELLMANN
Olympic Medalist, World Equestrian Games Winner, European Champion, German Champion

"The ability to adapt oneself to each horse is the prerequisite for success as a rider. Every horse is different. Horses are individuals, and therefore, the riding of each horse is a little different, even though we may all be following the principles of classical riding and the Training Scale. Respect for horses is expressed not only by caring for them in accordance with their nature, but also by individualized training, which improves their well-being."

MONICA THEODORESCU
Olympic Medalist, World Equestrian Games Winner, European Champion, German Champion

"The principles and concepts of dressage training are constant. But as a rider, one must be able to adapt to them. Each horse has different athletic abilities and a different personality, and this is what you must work with."

GEORGE WILLIAMS
US Dressage Team Member, President of the United States Dressage Federation (USDF)

"A horse cannot adapt himself to the rider. It is the rider's job to adapt himself to the horse. Every horse is different and one cannot work against the horse's nature. The rider must, using his own riding style, be able to adjust himself to each horse's unique traits in order to attain harmony."

KARIN REHBEIN
World Equestrian Games Winner, World-Class Trainer

"Each rider must have a guiding principle, a 'thread' that he follows. But within these guidelines it is important to adapt to every individual horse: his conformation and his character. Some horses must be ridden rounder and deeper while others must be ridden higher, and with others, more groundwork is the key to success. A riding stable is not a factory in which everything follows a set protocol."

JAN BRINK
Swedish Dressage Team Member, Reserve European Champion

"As a rider, you need a set of guidelines to follow to stay oriented. For me, this is the Training Scale. It lays out everything a rider needs to bring a horse along. Basically, I work all my horses in accordance with the Training Scale; however, there is always room for nuances so that different aspects of the Scale become more of a focus for certain horses based on their character and conformation."

HUBERTUS SCHMIDT
Olympic medalist, World Cup winner, European Champion, German Champion

"The rider is responsible for creating a 'team' with his horse. Thus, the rider must consider and recognize his horse's psychological and physical development. He must know his horse, and must study him and find out how much he can expect without overdoing it. He who ignores this will experience resistance and setbacks. We can't forget that not every horse can be brought to an *absolute* best, but taking his limitations into account, each horse can be brought to a *personal* best. For this reason, I prefer a horse with a good 'interior' over one with a good 'exterior.'"

JEAN BEMELMANS
Riding Master, Honorary Trainer in the DOKR (German Olympic Committee for Riding), World-Class Trainer, Chef d'Equipe of the Spanish Dressage Team

"A mistake made by many riders is to focus on high achievements in the show ring. I will admit I also have competitive ambitions. However, a satisfying partnership between horse and rider is a more important goal for me. This relationship can only be achieved when horse and rider trust and accept each other."

GÜNTHER FRÖHLICH
Friesian and Carriage Driving Expert

DETERMINING TYPE

While a horse owner may not possess the best horse in the world, the horse is likely wonderful in many ways despite his shortcomings—at least from the owner's subjective viewpoint. Ask any owner, and his or her "precious boy" or "girl" is probably "sensitive," "intelligent," or "simply charming." Even horses with conformational or character deficiencies receive such romanticized descriptions as "gorgeous," "unbelievably talented," or "just adorable." Here emerge the differences that make each horse unique in the eyes of his beholder, and they are not just due to the personal opinion of the owner—the differences are real. Horses are individuals and distinguish themselves through their character, their conformation, gender, pedigree, and breed. Anyone that has owned multiple horses or has ridden over a long period of time knows this well.

Perhaps your first horse was easy to handle and rarely put a foot wrong, while your second horse's stubborn demeanor had you at your wits' end. Horse Number Three was so different, he couldn't even be compared with the first two; despite—or perhaps because of—his sensitive nature, he was obedient and trustworthy. Such observations are the first step toward recognizing that no two horses are the same. And, by noticing these differences, you can learn something daily about handling and riding horses.

Both horses pictured here see something—note the difference! The top horse's expression is tense and agitated while the bottom horse is interested, yet relaxed.

WHAT'S "INSIDE"— WHAT MAKES MY HORSE DIFFERENT?

Look at your horse, observe the look in his eyes and his facial expression, as well as how he stands. This is all you need to get a glimpse into his character.

▸ Wide open eyes, actively swiveling ears, and flared nostrils often indicate a tendency toward fearfulness or nervousness. Such horses, in-hand and under saddle, often hold their head high in the air;

All three of these horses give the impression of a calm manner, but in slightly different ways.

they are on the lookout for danger and the fastest way to flee from it. Be prepared for overreaction!

► Half-closed, sleepy looking eyes indicate a calmer character. Combined with a somewhat sloppy stance, relaxed hanging ears, and even a shuffling gait, these horses are sluggish, phlegmatic, or at the very least what you might describe as "quiet" (note: this is not to be confused with stubbornness).

► Big eyes, ears that are usually pricked forward, an outstretched neck, and relaxed lips indicate curiosity and playfulness.

► Attentive ears combined with a "resting" hind leg indicate that the horse is alert to his surroundings, but calm at heart.

► The "skeptical" horse is often recognized from the ears and lips rather than the eyes. The ears are often back, the lips pressed together, and the nose wrinkled. This type of horse needs to be convinced of new things before he will cooperate.

These purely visual "type categories" can of course only show broad distinctions. There are many nuances within these groups, as well as combinations or overlapping of types. A horse can be fearful but also playful, curious but also skeptical. A tendency toward one character type does not rule out others. And, there are other issues that influence the nature of a horse. Whether a horse and rider get along and enjoy working together is determined by many factors.

WHAT'S "OUTSIDE"—HOW CONFORMATION AFFECTS THE HORSE

Conformation is an important factor influencing the harmony between horse and rider. When a horse is just living in a pasture, grazing all day, then it doesn't matter if his back is too long, his hind-quarters not properly angled, or his neck too short. But if the horse is to be ridden or competed, then these factors suddenly become important. The "stubborn nag" that is difficult to ride and unhappy in his work may not be able to accomplish a desired task because he doesn't have the physical prerequisites (in some cases, this can be rectified with correct training). For example, a horse with a short, steep shoulder cannot reach far in front of himself with his front legs. A horse with a low-set neck must be worked differently than one with an optimal neck position. A horse with an extremely long back will have difficulty "sitting down" behind in collected gaits, and a horse with small, weak hindquarters is not especially well suited to jumping. Young horses that grow in spurts over several years and also grow unevenly have difficulty balancing their developing bodies under the rider. The experienced rider knows to wait this out—the inexperienced or impatient rider wonders why the "stupid animal" has suddenly become so stubborn.

A horse's talent, ability to excel in his intended use, rideability, and learning ability depend on his physical structure as much as his attitude and personality. A horse with the most willing tempera-ment in the world cannot become a star if his conformation stands in his way. (This also applies to a still growing horse whose body is constantly changing.) The reverse is also true: The best rider cannot train a well built horse to be an Olympic winner if the horse lacks a good character. Sometimes a horse with a willing temperament but imperfect conformation can be brought to higher levels than a

A few of this horse's prominent conformational features—in his case, a somewhat low-set neck, and a short croup exaggerated by a big belly—could eventually lead to training difficulties.

horse with better conformation but a difficult demeanor. It is, of course, better and easier when both the conformation and character are good.

BREED DIFFERENCES

As discussed, character and conformation are two factors that contribute to making each horse unique. Additionally, breed characteristics play an important role. A Hanoverian or Dutch Warmblood, for example, will have a different disposition and appearance from a Friesian, Andalusian, or Thoroughbred. Of course their general "equine characteristics" are the same: They are all herd and flight animals; they all need forage such as hay or grass, and grain if they are in hard work (and more than likely, they all love to eat treats). Despite this there are important differences among the breeds that affect the horse's use as a riding horse—and especially as a dressage horse. Different breeds have different strengths and weaknesses, which must be considered when choosing a horse with a particular purpose in mind.

Let's consider, for example, Warmbloods: They have been bred in Europe as sport horses for generations to the extent that there are variations among the different Warmblood registries—for instance, Holsteiners are typically bred for jumping whereas Trakehners are bred for dressage. On the other hand, Friesians—recognizable by their naturally high neck set, luxurious manes, jet black coats, and

The long legs, spectacular movement, and general elegance of the Warmbloods we see in the dressage ring today are the result of carefully planned breeding.

A PRE stallion with training as a sport horse.

animated knee action—were originally bred to be carriage or parade horses. Recently, they have become very popular as riding horses, and many people have been training them as dressage prospects. This is not always an easy task since many Friesians do not have the ideal conformation for the sport. Their extremely high-set and thickly muscled neck must be worked deeper to improve the carrying capacity of their back, which is typically wide and slightly dipped. While every dressage horse must work on strengthening the back muscles, with Friesians it is especially important.

Some riders confuse the high-set neck of the Friesian with "upper level balance," and you often see horses at shows that are ridden too short in the neck with their hind legs trailing out behind them. A horse that is ridden with a too-short neck and dropped back will eventually develop riding and health problems. This need not always be the case with Friesians. If they are trained with a focus on improv-

ing the "swinging" of the back and encouraged to reach
forward and downward with the neck, Friesians, as well as other
horses with similar anatomical challenges, will only be limited by
the quality of their character, their gaits, and their talent. A Friesian
with a willing temperament, decent movement, and correct training
can even be as suitable for dressage as a Warmblood that is bred for
the sport. (However, Friesians are generally not ideal as jumpers or
event horses.)

With correct training that
takes their conformation
into account, talented
Friesians can be successful
in the dressage ring.

The good-natured and surefooted Haflinger is a popular pleasure horse in some countries.

The same is true for other Baroque breeds, such as the Andalusian/Pura Rasa Española (PRE) and Lusitano. Although recently emphasis has been placed on breeding a lighter type with conformation similar to the Warmblood, these horses remain endowed with powerful, high necks, short backs, and sloping shoulders, and so they must be worked slightly differently than horses with longer lines.

And, on a totally different scale, you might consider the "blonde" Haflinger. Due to their friendly nature, this breed is popular in some countries for riding and competing at the lower levels. Although recently lightened and refined, the Haflinger's strengths remain in being surefooted and uncomplicated rather than talented in dressage or jumping competition. Nonetheless, through appropriate classical training (as I discuss in this book), they can be worked within their limitations and become quite capable in various disciplines.

To return to character type for a moment (see p. 1), the modern Warmblood is often reputed to have a highly sensitive but somewhat difficult temperament. The Iberian breeds (Andalusians and Lusitanos) are thought to be uncomplicated, Friesians very friendly, and Thoroughbreds "hot." However, it is really impossible to make accurate sweeping generalizations about horse breeds, and their inborn riding qualities and nature. To describe horses only as "Friesians," "Andalusians," "Thoroughbreds," and "Warmbloods" is not sufficient. Within each breed there are many variations: horses with ideal and poor conformation, willing and unwilling temperaments, more or less intelligence, confidence or nervousness, stallion machismo and mare crankiness.

These last two varieties represent another important difference among horses: gender.

A Warmblood gelding—
a modern sport horse type.

Even at a young age, stallions...

MARE, STALLION, GELDING: WHAT ISSUES DOES GENDER POSE?

When evaluating a riding horse, the horse's gender plays a central role. The daily handling and riding of a mare is very different than that of a stallion. Mares can often be cranky, and while in heat they can be very "mareish"—generally more sensitive and less forgiving. Stallions often try to assert dominance. They want to be the boss in the stable, pasture, and under saddle. Geldings, with fewer hormones, tend not to exhibit these behaviors. Gender-specific problems usually do not apply to geldings. Most are quicker to forgive a riding error or misunderstanding, and they generally don't immediately take advantage of human weakness.

When a rider knows her horse well, she can usually tell the horse's mood by his or her facial expression. Mares tend to express a "bad mood" by laying back their ears, wrinkling their nose, swishing their tail, and maybe even nipping while being groomed or tacked-up. Stallions show off a "macho mood" by displaying imposing behavior, prancing around, whinnying, playful nipping, or dropping the penis.

...and mares are clearly distinguishable.

When a rider fights with a mare on the ground instead of remaining poised and confidently overlooking her moodiness, she will not have much fun in the saddle either. Remember the old adage "a mare is quick to take offense and slow to forgive." Therefore, as a rider, it is especially important to keep mares "on your side." Signs that a mare is unhappy in her work can include: increased tail swishing, kicking out in response to the leg or spur, and urinating while being ridden.

Stallions must also be handled and ridden in a special way. Because of their tendency toward dominance, it is important for the handler or rider to make it clear that she is in charge. Otherwise serious and dangerous incidents can occur. On the other hand, asserting leadership when working with a stallion should not be overdone as it can turn into an out-and-out fight. The rider should avoid turning a small dispute over rank into a big problem. When a fight occurs, there must naturally be a winner and a loser, and if the rider loses she can no longer trust the stallion because the stallion will not take her seriously. However, if the stallion loses, he might be ruined forever—broken spirited or dangerous. To avoid either catastrophe, be aware that the struggle over rank will likely be constant and it is best to solve incidents quickly and without a "winner" or "loser" if possible.

"TRUE" TYPES, "MADE" TYPES, "MIXED" TYPES

When contemplating a horse's type, it shouldn't be forgotten that some common horse "qualities" are actually created by people. Consider the "lazy horse," the "stubborn horse," the "resistant horse," and the "fearful horse." With correct and sensitive riding, these types might never come into being.

While *true types* are determined by inborn characteristics such as gender, breed, and conformation and cannot be changed, *made types* are the result of handler or rider error and can often be altered for the better.

We must not forget that no horse is characterized by only one type. Each horse is not only unique when compared to other horses, but is himself a complex life form that is influenced by many factors—a *mixed type*. These factors are so varied that when combined, the rider is constantly presented with a new challenge. For instance, a gelding can have a fearful nature but also be a sensitive and willing worker. Or he may be a beauty with ideal conformation but an erratic temperament, a lack of self-confidence, and a tendency to panic.

A single type can no more describe the complexity of a horse than a single training program can solve all the horse's problems. It would indeed be nice if riders could follow a simple recipe such as, "Take one hyperactive horse, add a calm rider, a dash of riding instructor, two teaspoons of Training Scale, and mix the ingredients together and let them sit for a few weeks." At the end, *voila*—you have a dream team.

It's just not that simple. (If it were, riding would probably be boring, wouldn't it?) The largest challenge lies in melding together the individuality of each horse and each rider.

WHICH TYPE AM I?

Every horse is different—but so is every rider. In order for horse and rider to form a harmonious pair, each rider must not only know her horse's type, but also her own type. In addition to technical riding skills, the rider needs physical, mental, strategic, and social skills in the saddle, all of which are interdependent.

A nervous rider would be advised not to choose a nervous horse. A petite rider with short legs will never achieve a deep seat on a big, wide horse. A rider that is equipped with little "feel" and body awareness will have difficulty on a hypersensitive horse, and one who is not yet familiar with movements and exercises will only experience frustration on an untrained or green horse. Only when the rider's skills and ability complement those of the horse does "teamwork" start to develop.

This rather small rider is well suited to her horse's build—she might find a bigger horse to be a more difficult ride.

RIDER PREREQUISITES

Interest in equestrian sports has steadily increased in the past few decades. Horse ownership has also increased. On the one hand, this is a positive step for the equestrian industry, but it also creates problems. Not every rider is equipped with the necessary skills to correctly ride her horse without instruction, and even fewer are prepared to train a horse. Often enthusiastic but inexperienced riders are keen to have a horse of their own, and they very frequently choose a young and therefore inexperienced horse. In such a scenario, the rider's limits are quickly exceeded by the horse and sooner or later problems ensue. Even green riders who wisely buy a trained horse cannot advance, or will get "stuck" at a certain point, without the help of an experienced trainer. A horse is not like a car that once tuned up doesn't change—training and good riding, daily or at least regularly, are prerequisites for both horse and rider to enjoy the riding experience.

Correct training is necessary for both rider and horse to enjoy the riding experience.

GROUNDWORK

Correct riding in accordance with the Training Scale (see p. 17) implies work under saddle. This, however, doesn't mean that work appropriate to your horse's type can't be accomplished via other means—namely, groundwork. For every different horse type, how the horse should be handled on the ground varies: Handling of nervous horses manifests itself differently from that of calm ones; handling fresh horses differs from handling quiet ones; and working with geldings is different from work with  stallions. Some horses require more purposeful groundwork (exercises and the like) whereas for others, normal daily handling is sufficient. When a horse trusts people and takes them seriously on the ground, his ridden work always improves.

On one side of the equation is the training of the horse, and on the other (and no less importantly) is the training of the rider. A correct seat and position, clear administration of the aids, and therefore effectiveness in the saddle, can take years for the rider to learn, and even then must be constantly checked, corrected, and fine-tuned. Everything that the rider does has an effect on the horse—both the correct and the incorrect.

Riding according to a horse's individual type is highly demanding and tests the skill of the rider. The more capable the rider, the more exactly she will be able to attend to her horse's particular needs. It is possible that the "made" horse types I mentioned earlier (see p. 12)—"the lazy horse," "the stubborn horse," and "the fearful horse," for example—would never be created if riders paid as much attention to their own training and advancement as to that of their horse.

Every horse, regardless of breed or discipline (with the exception of competitive racehorses), can and should be trained in accordance with the dressage Training Scale (see p. 17). Sentiments such as

A Horses need ample time to run free in the pasture, as well as...

B ...cavaletti work, jumping gymnastics,...

A CHANGE IN ROUTINE

Regardless of which type of horse one has, variety in daily work is always beneficial. By changing up the routine, the lazy, dull horse is refreshed and finds enjoyment in his work again, and the nervous horse can find busywork to focus on and help him relax. Instead of monotony, riding can be continuously fun for horse and rider. Dressage work mixed with jumping gymnastics, cavaletti, longeing, trail riding, and—of course—ample turnout can combine to create a happy horse.

"Dressage training isn't really worth it," are nonsense. Dressage training is always worthwhile and is also our duty as riders as it preserves the health and athleticism of the horse.

Of course one could pose the question as to whether it is worthwhile, for example, for a top-level rider to spend time training a horse with limited capabilities. From the perspective of the rider, probably not, but for the horse it is definitely worth it. The horse can be significantly improved even with his limitations and can then bring a lot of joy to a less competitively oriented rider. On the other hand, many horses are more capable than their rider but do not advance be-

C ...and relaxing rides in the countryside.

cause the rider fails to recognize the horse's potential or invest in his training. Some riders blame the horse for their failures without ever looking to themselves for the source of the problem, and so exchange the horse for another, and another, and another.

THE TRAINING SCALE

Rhythm, suppleness and relaxation, contact, impulsion, straightness, and collection—these are the six pillars of the Training Scale. From my perspective, it is pointless to debate whether the Training Scale is meaningful for every horse, or whether suppleness and relaxation should be addressed before rhythm, as critics of the Scale often propose, or whether the concepts of balance, "throughness," and harmony should be explicitly included.

The Training Scale is the only systematic training methodology that is ultimately determined by the horse. It is not a rigid framework but a flexible construct that can be applied to any type of horse. The points of the Training Scale occur in succession and are intertwined and interrelated. Depending on the type of horse you have, one

A horse that is trained in adherence to the Training Scale without the use of force should, like La Picolina, be as rideable bareback with nothing but a halter and lead rope to guide her as she is with saddle and double bridle.

aspect of the Training Scale can sometimes come into play a little early or become slightly more important than another. However, the "big picture" always remains the same, because only a horse that is trained according to the Training Scale will develop true balance under saddle. Correct training ultimately rewards the rider with "throughness" (the horse is connected from back to front, displays no signs of resistance, and responds willingly to the slightest of rider aids), the prerequisite for lightness and harmony to develop between horse and rider, whether in the dressage ring, on a jumping course, or out on the trail.

Depending on the type of horse, sometimes problems (some small and others large) will have to be worked through before each pillar of the Training Scale is mastered. With an optimal horse, an optimal rider, and optimal training, problems would probably never occur—but how often is everything optimal? In real life the rider must deal with the few or many shortcomings of his horse and of himself. But, this should never be an excuse for diverting from the time-tested and proven benefits of the Training Scale.

"Throughness," harmony, and a relaxed, swinging back are not dependent on a bit, reins, and knee rolls. La Picolina and I enjoy testing our connection by schooling with minimal tack.

NADINE CAPELLMANN AND FARBENFROH

"My most unusual horse was definitely Farbenfroh. His temperament was actually quite good; he was neither too hot nor too lazy. However, he was extremely 'looky.' It was very hard for the rider to adjust to his 'looking' because he would sometimes shy and sometimes not. I never knew when or where he was going to see something that would cause him to stop or startle. It was at times something in the distance, but more frequently an object on the ground. Farbenfroh was extremely skeptical of things on the ground. For example, when we started competing at bigger shows, he had a problem with the freshly rolled centerline. So my trainer at the time, Klaus Balkenhol, rolled out centerline after centerline in our arena at home, until Farbenfroh eventually learned not to let this 'strange sand formation' ruin his composure.

"At the time we also did a lot of groundwork using the Tellington Method® (www.tellingtonttouch.com) to address his shying and lack of confidence. We would put flower pots in new places, hang a blanket over the arena fence, or lay a sheet of plastic on the ground and ask him to walk over it. After a while, Farbenfroh began to really enjoy this groundwork—it was like a big playground for him. We spent two to three years doing this regularly while also constantly changing the surroundings when he was ridden. When he would 'look' at something, I would praise and pet him but also use driving aids to ride him past the 'obstacle.'

"It's very important that while the rider does not use force in these situations, she still follows through and accomplishes the task at hand. Farbenfroh had to learn to be obedient to the rider's aids, and in the process, he realized that most of the things he wanted to shy at actually weren't that scary. Therefore, my main focus was on basic gymnasticizing while improving obedience and 'throughness' (see p. 19). Over time he greatly reduced his 'looking' and the little that remained was not so hard to deal with (in general, it should be made clear that 'lookiness' can usually be brought under control by improving 'throughness')."

Nadine Capellmann
and Farbenfroh were a
"dream team."

"In addition, a rider must know his horse well and know what he is afraid of in order to guide him in a calm and relaxed but logical way. Care should be taken that the training doesn't compound the problem resulting in an even tenser horse. The horse must know that he can rely on his rider in critical situations. The biggest mistake in such situations is to put the horse under too much pressure because that starts a vicious cycle that becomes increasingly harder to break. But it is also incorrect to allow a horse to be 'looky' and do nothing about it. Then the habit progresses until it is so bad that you can only ride your horse in a small circle in the middle of the arena! The secret lies in finding a balance that preserves your horse's trust in you while being determined enough to accomplish your task."

CHARACTER TYPES

Isabell Werth and Satchmo.

INDIVIDUAL DIFFERENCES

As we've discussed, no two horses are the same. The individual differences lie in "outside" characteristics (conformation, breed, gender) and in character types—what's "inside." The following character overview is by no means all-encompassing, but rather broadly covers major points. I hope that readers will be able to recognize some of their horse's traits within the generalized categories in this section.

THE HYPER OR OVERREACTIVE HORSE

Hyper or overreactive horses can usually be identified by their tendency to dance around and their lack of calmness during the grooming, saddling, and mounting process. This type of horse is nervous and uncertain, and usually exhibits his inner tension by sweating quickly and heavily during work. Such horses are pre-programmed for overreaction, in daily handling as well as under saddle.

In training, hyper horses have difficulty with specific elements of the Training Scale: rhythm, suppleness and relaxation, and contact. A lack of what we might call "inner peace" makes it hard for these horses to concentrate. This can result in a loss of rhythm, increased tension, head tossing, and ultimately slower learning, which in turn has a negative effect on the development and improvement of impulsion, straightness, and collection.

Common Training Mistakes
Reacting with pressure (i.e. harsher aids, draw reins, punishment) and impatience due to time deadlines is absolutely counterproductive with this type of horse.

Training Tips
A hyper horse can only be helped by an experienced, completely calm and relaxed rider who is patient and lets nothing ruin her composure. (Actually, this is a character description that *every* rider should

have!) The rider must take the horse's negative tension and apply it to something positive so that the horse feels secure.

If possible, hyper horses should be longed for 10 to 20 minutes before they are ridden so that they can move forward without being restricted by the rider. This usually succeeds in starting to relax the horse. Then the horse should be calmly led to the arena, where the rider mounts, although if the horse becomes nervous again, then an assistant should hold the horse in order to prevent a fight between horse and rider from starting in the early moments of the ride. The hyper horse—nervous and uncertain—becomes even more agitated in anticipation of further conflict with his rider. An assistant on the ground gives the horse security and ensures that once the rider mounts, a battle will not immediately ensue. (Note: While tips like these may sound trivial, they are extremely valuable in ensuring a relaxed interaction with a horse with a hyper tendency.)

Hyper horses commonly overreact to aspects of their surroundings. They think great danger lurks behind every bush.

In all my experience as a rider and trainer, the most extreme case of a hyper horse I have dealt with was my chestnut gelding, Allegro. He was a meek, affectionate, but nervous horse, who I lovingly referred to as "Sweetie," but to others was known as "Psycho." He came to me as a three year old, having previously lived in a field with other young horses at his breeder's farm. This is generally the best way for young horses to develop psychologically, but apparently, in Allegro's case, his genes stood in his way. He was tentative, quick to panic, and very jumpy—character traits that hugely influenced his training. I ended up in the hospital three times after falling from him (one of these times, embarrassingly, was at a horse show). I attempted to gain support by putting him in training with an experienced professional, but the idea failed after only a few weeks, with the trainer and Allegro at their wits' end. And, due to a lack of proper progressive training, Allegro ended up twice in a row with tendon injuries necessitating lengthy recoveries. I tried all manner of different things, but Allegro overreacted to everything and was always resistant, only spiraling deeper into his uncertainty. Even seemingly simple exercises like the leg-yield completely unnerved him. Later on, it took him two full years to learn canter pirouettes.

By nature, hyper horses have the most difficulty with the second element of the Training Scale: suppleness and relaxation. Horses

HYPER HORSES NEED TIME

Hyper, nervous horses need especially calm and relaxed riders who are willing to devote much time to general handling. The rider should avoid moving quickly or hurrying when around her horse, and she should refrain from yelling or being otherwise loud in order to prevent communicating stress to the horse. Never saddle this kind of horse when under time constraints. Extensive grooming in combination with Tellington TTouches® (www.tellingtonttouch.com) or other relaxation techniques are helpful. Overreactive horses require strict and clear handling on the ground, since they tend to be uncertain and therefore benefit from leadership.

like this—and Allegro was no exception—are always on the go and constantly on the lookout for perceived danger. They often want to do everything right and become completely stressed by small mistakes, unclear aids from the rider, or outside distractions.

When training a hyper horse, building trust and relaxation is of the utmost importance. Without trusting his rider the horse will neither find his rhythm nor accept contact with the rider's hand. He is quick to notice mistakes, weakness, or uncertainty on the rider's part and reacts by becoming increasingly difficult to ride, and eventually resistant.

Successfully achieving suppleness and relaxation without disregarding rhythm and contact depends on the horse's age, his level of training, and the capabilities of the rider. For a young horse of this type or a nervous horse under an inexperienced rider, auxiliary reins—ideally, Vienna reins—can be helpful. When used correctly, they give the horse and rider a small amount of psychological security. (Alternatively, a running martingale can be used.)

In the long run, it is the goal to do without auxiliary reins, but for critical or difficult situations, they can be very helpful. When used correctly, they "even out" the rider's aids and thus encourage the horse to trust his rider more and feel a bit more secure—this is the basis for physical and mental relaxation and thus the first step *away* from the overreactive behavior. If the horse is not relaxed he will always react poorly to new requests from the rider. This then can become a downward spiral. Relaxation is required for developing concentration in *all* horses, not just hyper ones, and concentration is a prerequisite for learning.

Just as nervous human athletes can improve their performance using relaxation and concentration techniques such as yoga, horses can also benefit from similar methods—Tellington TTouch® is one that can be used daily. The rider doesn't need to follow a complicated routine to help the horse relax. Simply patting the horse before mounting, scratching him a little on the withers, or perhaps always riding 20 minutes at the walk at the beginning of a ride is enough to give the horse the extra security he needs.

During a work session, the addition of the individual gaits and movements must be very selectively handled. Because the hyper horse is nervous and overreacts, he is quick to become tense again even after you've calmed him down. In the warm-up phase, the rider must try to lull the horse a little: instead of riding at a very forward pace, trot a little under tempo. Ride frequent transitions to walk (not

Allegro could look spectacular but the pressure of professional training was too much for him. Note his facial expression and the look in his eyes. His ears are back and his nostrils are flared.

Allegro again under less pressure—perhaps he doesn't look quite as spectacular but instead he has a satisfied facial expression.

to halt, as this can increase tension) and walk for longer periods in between the other gaits. Ride many school figures and bending lines to increase the horse's concentration. Only when the horse is no longer distracted by every outside noise but is instead paying attention to the rider is it time to ride a little more forward and introduce changes of pace, without losing the suppleness and relaxation gained.

While this "anti-hyper work" takes effect, the basis for the other two foundation elements of the Training Scale, rhythm and contact, will be solidified. Correct rhythm in the gaits is often lacking in over-reactive horses more than other types of horses. Their lack of supple-ness and relaxation affects the other points on the Scale. Deficits in these areas can prevent a horse from advancing, not necessarily in terms of competition, but rather as a satisfied riding horse that in turn brings his rider satisfaction. Thus when dealing with a hyper horse, it is crucial to devote a lot of time and patience to the quest for suppleness and relaxation. While it is the trickiest, it is also the most important.

When the rider has taken time to focus on the basic elements of the Training Scale, then the foundation is properly laid for those that remain. However, the hyper horse will always require his rider to take steps back and return to the basics. If this is not done faith-fully it will eventually be detrimental to the horse's psychological well-being.

Allegro, by the way, with all his delays and detours, did win at FEI-level dressage. And before he went into early retirement due to a lung problem, he once again taught me the importance of patience.

THE SLOW OR STOLID HORSE

"If you can't come today, just come tomorrow," sums up the outlook of the slow, stolid horse. This type of horse doesn't let anything un-settle him. Because he tends not to be spooky, he is a good match for beginners or fearful riders. However, if this state of calm oversteps a healthy limit, it can easily become laziness and extreme dullness to the rider's aids, which negatively influences the horse's rideability and his ability to ascend the Training Scale.

Common Training Mistakes
There are two big mistakes that are made with this kind of horse. The first is to allow sluggish behavior to occur in daily handling from the ground. It is quite typical for the rider of such a slow, impassive

THE IMPORTANCE OF DISCIPLINE

Handling a slow, stolid horse has its own set of problems. While you don't have to worry that the horse will suddenly startle and run you over, you must keep in mind that he very well might step on your foot and remain calmly standing on it, despite your efforts to dislodge him! This kind of horse enjoys being relaxed, and knows how to shamelessly take advantage of situations in order to stay that way. Starting with his everyday handling on the ground, his handler must give very clear commands and insist that they are followed immediately. If this is not done, the horse will learn that his handler need not be taken seriously, which then carries over to work under saddle. After all, why should the horse be sensitive to commands under saddle when he isn't expected to be in other situations?

mount to *pull* his horse out of the stall or to the riding arena, rather than lead him correctly with the horse walking actively and respectfully at his side. Then, once the rider is in the saddle, the horse barely awakes from his lethargy. And why should he? The half-asleep behavior had been fully tolerated on the ground. The second mistake is to lack a logical plan for discipline when the rider's aids are ignored, thereby gradually making the horse progressively duller to them (see more about this below).

Training Tips

The slow, stolid horse needs an especially disciplined person, who gives all commands, whether on the ground or in the saddle, very clearly, and insists that the horse respond correctly and instantly. If allowed, this type of horse will quickly find the easy way out. As mentioned, what is often initially perceived to be calmness and quietness can easily become "deadness to the leg aids," turning the riding experience into little more than constant kicking and repetitive application of the spurs. Over time, this only teaches the horse to further ignore the leg aids and makes him even more "behind the leg." This, in turn, has a negative effect on the horse's rhythm, causing the horse to lose the proper number of beats in all three gaits. Rhythm irregularities creep in at the trot, while the three beats of the canter become four, and what should be a clear, four-beat walk becomes a pace.

Impulsion—which can be described as the energetic impulse generated by the hindquarters that is released into forward movement at the trot and canter—cannot be accomplished when rhythm is disrupted and the horse is dull to the leg aids. Straightness is compromised, as well as collection (which, at best, will be expressed as a slow shuffle rather than an expressive cadenced movement).

To prevent the situation from deteriorating to this point, the rider must make a concerted effort to "wake up" the horse and gain his attention. A small but important detail is to always lead the horse at a brisk pace. If necessary, a whip can be carried while leading so it is on-hand to tap the horse on the hindquarters and drive him forward as necessary. Leading in an energetic manner increases the horse's focus on his handler so he is prepared for further commands. The

When the horse doesn't take his handler seriously, green grass is far more important than obedience to the handler's cues.

same applies when riding at the walk at the beginning of a work session. The horse should march forward willingly and not laze along unenthusiastically while the rider is lost in her thoughts or chats with a friend. The more forward energy generated (note: the pace should *not* be hurried), the better you can avoid the rhythm problems I mentioned on p. 30.

In order to get a horse "in front of the leg" it is very important to apply your leg aid only for a short duration, with only as much pressure as necessary, and to get the required response from the horse. If a light squeeze with the calves is not enough to motivate the horse then the rider is justified in giving one or two more "energetic" leg aids. If necessary, these may need to be applied in conjunction with a tap of the whip. If the horse then reacts by going forward as requested, then he must be *allowed* to move forward and praised immediately. "Kicking and pulling" at the same time is fundamentally incorrect and will only confuse the horse.

Slow, impassive-type horses should be often ridden very forward in order to wake them up, focus their attention on the rider, and ac-

> ### THE DRIVING LEG—
> ### A COMMONLY MISUNDERSTOOD AID
>
> The concept of the driving leg aid has different interpretations. It is often confused with constantly squeezing or gripping with the legs. But, actual "driving" has nothing to do with this.
>
> Instead, it should be a skillful combination of seat and leg aids. The seat aid is a result of a balanced upper body position with a freely moving pelvis, which has a continuous effect on the horse. The driving leg aid is nothing other than a touch of the leg, applied as needed—when not in use the leg should hang re-relaxed at the horse's side.
>
> The driving leg can be used on one side or both, and it can serve to send the horse forward or sideways. The more sensitive the horse is to the leg, the more subtly the leg aid can be applied. With highly trained horse, just "thinking" of the aid or "breathing" with your leg will suffice. On the other hand, when a horse is not sensitive to the leg or has been made dull to the aids by a rider constantly gripping with her heels or digging with her spurs, a quick energetic kick will have to be used to reinstate a proper response from the horse. It is then crucial to allow the horse to move forward (the desired response) and to immediately praise him.

custom them to the feel of movement with impulsion. Supporting exercises include frequent changes of pace within the gait (lengthening and collecting), as well as simple suppling exercises such as circles, voltes, serpentines, changes of direction, and leg-yield. Riding such exercises avoids monotony and keeps the horse's attention. In addition, riding in the two-point position over cavalletti and gymnastics, and regular trail rides, help keep the horse mentally and physically fresh so he enjoys his work.

When the horse stays "on the aids"—and remains sensitive to the leg aids, especially—then he will react with a "quicker" hind leg—one that steps further under the body and doesn't trail behind. This is a prerequisite for collection. In contrast, if the horse reacts to the aids incorrectly, or doesn't react at all, then the rider must immediately give a concise but meaningful reminder. This does not mean kicking every stride, raking with the spurs, or gripping tightly with the calves. Said plainly, the aid should amount to a quick "kick-kick," repeated twice if necessary with the heel or spur. When the horse reacts with forward movement, the rider should praise him. This is the way to keep the slow, stolid horse "quick off the leg" and, therefore, more sensitive.

Sensitivity to the rider's aids is of utmost importance, because without this *nothing* can be easy and harmonious: flying changes, transitions, canter pirouettes, and piaffe will all be strained, if not impossible. Hunters, jumpers, and event horses must be sensitive to the aids in order to maneuver through technically difficult courses. Whatever your discipline, your safety and success depends upon this factor.

These two gymnastic lines are suitable for horses of all different types and offer a fun training alternative to schooling on the flat. The first line is easier to ride and is ideal as an introduction. The second line, in addition to being fun for the horse, builds his strength and flexibility and increases his ability to react.

GYMNASTICS TO "AWAKEN" AND "REFRESH" THE HORSE

APPROACH IN TROT

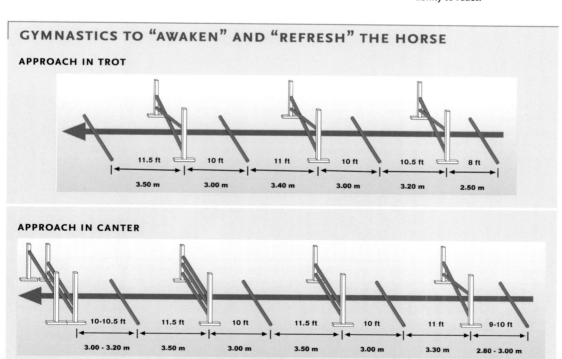

| 11.5 ft | 10 ft | 11 ft | 10 ft | 10.5 ft | 8 ft |
| 3.50 m | 3.00 m | 3.40 m | 3.00 m | 3.20 m | 2.50 m |

APPROACH IN CANTER

| 10-10.5 ft | 11.5 ft | 10 ft | 11.5 ft | 10 ft | 11 ft | 9-10 ft |
| 3.00 - 3.20 m | 3.50 m | 3.00 m | 3.50 m | 3.00 m | 3.30 m | 2.80 - 3.00 m |

(Exercises recommended by Alois Pollmann-Schweckhorst, author of *Training the Modern Jumper*)

THE "HOT" HORSE

This type of horse is most recognizable by his enormous urge to go forward, paired with latent nervousness, which presents itself as "running under saddle." Many Thoroughbreds and Thoroughbred-crosses, especially, are "hot" as their genes carry with them a desire to run. In general this type of horse is a willing worker, but due to his fiery temperament, he has difficulty with the Training Scale elements of rhythm, suppleness and relaxation, and—most of all—contact. He tends to become too short in the neck, pull against the rider's hands, or toss his head.

While hot horses struggle with many aspects of training for dressage or pleasure, when handled well, they can be especially successful. They are often misjudged and handled inappropriately. For example, in an effort to calm the horse, many riders incessantly "ride the brakes," meaning they continuously pull back on the reins. The hot horse wants to (and by his nature *must*) move forward, but in such a case is forcefully prevented from acting according to his disposition. This creates an explosive situation that can lead to mul-

This attractive but hot mare tends to want to "run away" under saddle. As a result she becomes too short in the neck and pulls down on the contact.

tifaceted problems. The more the horse tries to run, the more the rider pulls on the reins, causing the horse to want to run even more, and leading to disrupted rhythm in all three gaits, and a mentally stressed and physically tense horse that will never relax or become supple. Eventually, in order to escape the uncomfortable and unceasing pressure on the reins, the horse will have problems with contact, which will manifest itself as head tossing or another such issue.

In addition, development of true impulsion, which relies on a "swinging" back, will be impossible, straightness will be compromised, and collection will be expressed, at best, as spectacular "leg flinging" rather than easy, dancer-like steps. To top it off, in this scenario, "throughness" (see p. 19) is completely unattainable.

Common Training Mistakes

The worst thing the rider can do with a hot horse is use force (extremely short reins, constant rein pressure, draw reins) to contain the horse's forward desire. You can often see riders on hot horses with their lower leg stretched away off the horse's side. This only makes the situation worse, not better.

By riding bending lines and lots of school figures, the hot mare begins to relax.

Riding calmly in shoulder-in helps bring this mare's urge to run forward under control.

Training Tips

Like the hyper, overreactive horse (see p. 23), the hot horse does best with an experienced, patient, and calm rider. Only such a rider can ensure that the horse becomes relaxed enough in warm-up that his schooling session will improve his rideability and, eventually, his "throughness." In order to avoid or correct consistent "running away" under saddle, the hot horse, again like the hyper horse, can be longed before the rider mounts. This way the horse's desire to really move can be indulged without the rider on his back. There are a few fundamental points that the rider must be aware of:

1. She must ride with longer reins than she would instinctively think necessary.
2. She must keep her calves lightly on the horse's sides rather than stretching them away in an attempt to not make contact.
3. She must correct the horse's pace and tempo within each gait with her seat and weight aids, rather than her reins.
4. She should ride without a whip, if possible.

Many riders find the first point a tough one since they tend to automatically use the reins as brakes. This reaction, however—as already mentioned—causes the horse to run even more. In contrast, a longer rein allows the horse to relax his neck and stretch it forward and down toward the connection with the rider's hand—prerequisites for attaining a raised and "swinging" back. In this "long-and-low" position, the horse can better relax his body and avoid painful muscle cramping. Only when the hot horse's body is relaxed is he able to concentrate on the rider's aids.

The second point addresses the rider's lower leg. Many riders think that taking the legs *off* the horse will stop him or slow him down. The opposite is the case. A leg that lightly lies on the horse's side (but not gripping!) stabilizes the rider's position and allows her to sit with her upper body balanced on the vertical. When the lower leg is stretched away from the horse the rider becomes unbalanced and can easily fall behind the vertical—a position that puts too much pressure on the horse's back and causes the horse to try to run forward out from under the discomfort. The light touch of the rider's legs on the horse's sides gives the horse a feeling of security, and from this position the leg aids can be applied quietly and subtly without surprise. When the leg aids arrive out of nowhere it alarms the horse.

The best way to regulate the horse's tempo (the rate of repetition of the rhythm) is with weight aids, and this is most easily done in

CALMING SUPPLEMENTS

Correct feed and nutrition can have a positive influence on a hot horse. The addition of natural and legal dietary supplements or herbal remedies has been seen by some to be of benefit. Certain pheromones and fragrances are also known to have a relaxing effect. Even though such supplements should pose no harm to the horse's health, their use should be discussed with a trusted veterinarian. It is important to administer the correct dose and to avoid feeding too much or an incorrect combination of ingredients.

Please note I do not advise the use of so-called "calming" medication or drugs.

CALM THE HORSE BY EXERCISING HIS MIND

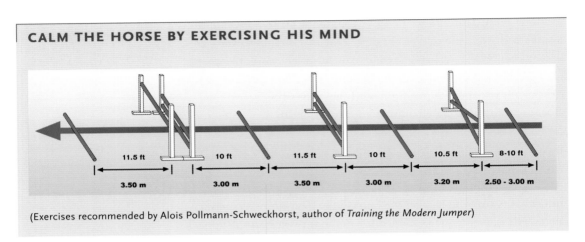

| 11.5 ft | 10 ft | 11.5 ft | 10 ft | 10.5 ft | 8-10 ft |

| 3.50 m | 3.00 m | 3.50 m | 3.00 m | 3.20 m | 2.50 - 3.00 m |

(Exercises recommended by Alois Pollmann-Schweckhorst, author of *Training the Modern Jumper*)

For a horse that tends to be hot, the best gymnastic line is short with a ground pole after the last fence, so that the horse's speed can be regulated at the end of the line.

rising trot. The rider must try to "sit" a little longer than the horse's tempo dictates, and when in the upbeat of posting, the rider must try to stay out of the saddle slightly longer before sitting in the saddle again. This causes the rider to be slightly behind the rhythm of the horse, which feels strange to the rider, but also to the horse. Almost all horses respond by slowing their tempo, and this is achieved without pulling or force. This method of effectively "sitting against" the horse's movement can also help slow a too-quick canter.

A hurried walk can be made slowed with several methods. Some horses react well when the rider half-halts for several strides or when the rider asks for a full halt, waits for a moment, and then allows the horse to move forward again. Other horses react better to small school figures, such as voltes and serpentines, or to leg-yield. While practicing these simple exercises, the rider should apply half-halts

By using her seat and weight, "sitting" against the horse's movement, and half-halting, this rider gains her mare's attention and keeps her from speeding up and pulling down against her hands.

and the aids for flexion, which increase the horse's concentration and his acceptance of the driving leg aids (see p. 32).

As I have mentioned, many people are confused by the application of driving leg aids on a hot horse because they believe that using leg on a hot horse is counterproductive. A driving leg, however, does not have to result in running the horse forward, but instead it can harness the impulsion from the hind legs, "driving" it over the horse's back and into the rider's hand; thus encouraging the horse to "chew the reins out of the rider's hands" and let his neck drop forward and down. The result of this exercise is relaxation of the body and mind.

Riding simple school figures combined with half-halts, as well as shoulder-fore and shoulder-in, increases the horse's focus on the rider, allows the horse to relax, and teaches the horse to "stay with the rider" rather than running out from under her. This provides the rider the opportunity to apply driving leg aids while the horse is attentive.

Halting for lengthy periods of time is difficult for hot horses and should only be practiced when the horse can remain calm at all three gaits. If the horse insists on dancing around at the halt, the rider must not lose her calm. Rough "correction" from the rider, such as jerking on the reins or kicking the horse in irritation, only makes the horse never want to stand still because he anticipates punishment. Instead, it often helps to loosen the reins while halted, even if the contact is lost. Rubbing the horse on the neck or behind the saddle helps to relax both horse and rider. Sometimes it even helps if the rider thinks about something completely different from halting, or the movement just completed, or riding at all! When the rider relaxes subconsciously it often carries over to the horse.

When the horse learns to trust his rider and wait for her aids, then training can proceed to the next level. Patience and calmness is, therefore, imperative with hot horses. As with hyper horses (see p. 23), riders of hot horses must consciously focus on the basics— particularly suppleness and relaxation. Relaxation is an extremely fragile state in these horses and can easily be distorted or destroyed by incorrect riding. This includes position flaws such as leaning too far back; an unbalanced or stiff seat; unsteady hands; roughly applied aids; and can be exacerbated by poor choices of exercises and movements. The latter can be easily corrected with a little thought. For example, many horses become quite excited when one movement is repeated in quick succession. Five simple changes at the end of the diagonal, or 20 rein-backs in a row, are inappropriate choices for schooling a hot horse. Here the saying "less is more" is relevant.

The same can be applied to riding out on the trail. The rider should vary the location where he asks the horse for a brisk canter so that the horse does not learn to anticipate. The horse should be given calming walk breaks combined with stints of rising trot before cantering again.

When the hot horse has relaxed and accepts the rider's aids, half-steps—shortened trot steps with a reduced phase of suspension—can be added to the training program. Half-steps improve the horse's carrying power. The hot horse's strong "go forward" impulse is very helpful for this exercise.

MONICA THEODORESCU AND ARAK

"Over the years I have had many different horses to ride, but the most unique was definitely my Thoroughbred, Arak. As an ex-racehorse, he came to me with completely different past experiences than all my other horses. He never received basic dressage training like other horses of his age. Nonetheless, due to his excellent nature and intelligence, he was able to learn quite quickly.

"I still remember how flying changes were such a challenge for him. Especially later, when he was trying to learn one-tempi changes, he could get really, really 'fast.' It seemed like it reminded him of his racing career. For a time we emphasized this movement—not with unending repetition, but simply by focusing on the change itself. My father (Riding Master Georg Theodorescu) was always of the opinion that when a horse learns a new and difficult movement, his mind shouldn't be burdened with too many other movements. Many riders make the mistake of introducing a new movement at the very end of a training session. But by this point the horse's mind and body are usually tired and his capacity to learn is diminished. It is wiser to introduce a new movement in the middle of the ride.

"So, I would warm Arak up normally: a relaxed warm-up phase followed by a little gymnasticizing work in trot and canter and the occasional flying change. As soon as he was loosened up we started—indirectly—working on the changes in sequence. I schooled this by riding simple changes from one lead to the other in quick succession, so that he was repeatedly picking up a new canter lead. When he did this well, I would let him do flying changes, and then eventually ask for two one-tempis in a row. As soon as this was completed correctly, my father would let me praise him, dismount, loosen the girth, and end the day's work session. We progressively proceeded in the same manner, and Arak eventually learned to calmly do three, then four one-tempis in succession. Once he learned to do four, the movement 'clicked' for him, and he understood what was being asked.

"Even today, I use this same method of training when a horse has a problem with flying changes, and especially one-tempis. As soon as the horse does the desired movement correctly, I dismount, praise the horse, give him a treat, loosen the girth, and lead him back to the stable. My father believed that the horse takes a positive learning experience like this with him and thinks about it afterward. It may sound strange, but I think it's true.

"I can definitely say that we never had a horse that didn't quickly learn one-tempis using this method, and without stress, as well. It worked extremely well for Arak, in particular. He was hot—a *really* hot horse—but once he grasped a concept, the rider only had to push the button. His trouble with suppleness and relaxation early in training was solved with continuous gymnasticizing work, including frequent transitions, serpentines, and voltes, so that eventually it was no longer an issue at all."

The Thoroughbred Arak started his career as a racehorse and then became a successful Grand Prix dressage horse.

THE PRANKSTER

It is hard to believe, but even horses can be pranksters. These horses are often geldings or stallions that are highly self-confident, curious, and playful, plus have a macho side and are naturally mischievous. They are often extremely dominant types that always look to challenge the rider with a "discussion" of sorts, depending on the "topic" at hand. The prankster likes to learn and advance in his training, and is also the sort that enjoys learning tricks and "getting into trouble" in his daily life.

Common Training Mistakes

To laugh everything off with an, "Oh, isn't that cute!" is just as incorrect as trying to nip every little action in the bud. Zombie-like obedience is not likely with this type of horse, and if insisted upon, can take away the horse's individual "spark" and charm.

Training Tips

Day-to-day riding practice and (especially) the initial basic training of a prankster presents perpetual challenges for the rider. Generally, this type of horse learns quite quickly; however, they are also quick to learn undesirable things—much more than other types of horses. The prankster's inborn curiosity makes him an intelligent partner that never stops observing his rider or handler and happily testing him on a variety of subjects. This intelligence, on the other hand, also makes working with these horses so appealing.

ALLOW THE HORSE TO PLAY

In addition to structured albeit forgiving handling, pranksters need to be kept busy. They have a strong desire to play that must be fulfilled. A toy such as a Jolly Ball® or a tree branch in the horse's stall or paddock keeps him mentally busy and out of trouble. Creating variety in ridden work should be a priority. If time permits, pranksters love to learn tricks; a few well-chosen ones can be fun for both horse and rider.

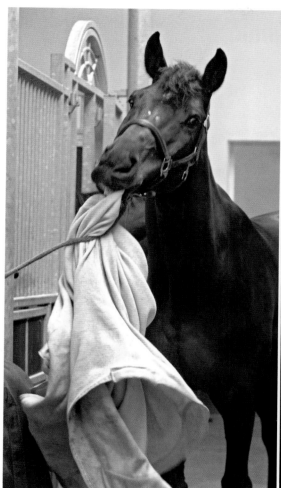 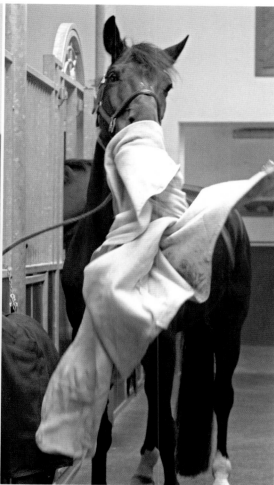

Nothing is safe when "Büffel," a
real prankster, is around!

Assuming the prankster has no extreme conformational weaknesses and is worked correctly, his character does not predispose him
to any difficulties with particular elements of the Training Scale (as
we've seen with some of the other types). The prankster's greatest
problem is his tendency to mercilessly take advantage of any uncertainty or mistake made by the rider and to react with mischief or bla-
tant disobedience and resistance.

I have encountered varying degrees of prankster behavior in the
course of my riding career. So far the king of them all is my young

Here shown with his ears pricked forward and an attentive facial expression, the prankster "Büffel" is usually in a good mood and often has jokes and general clowning around on his mind. This is exactly the charm of this type of horse, and what we must strive to preserve.

horse, Courbière, who is better known by his nickname "Büffel" (buffalo). This 17.3-hand gelding has a very friendly, curious, and brave nature but also has a tendency to be extremely mischievous. Nothing is secure or sacred when Büffel is around; everything ends up in his mouth and is carried around or somehow rearranged. He enjoys tearing stable blankets, tipping over full wheelbarrows, and emptying out brush boxes. And, once he realized that the person on the other end of the longe line was nowhere near as strong as he, he began to throw his enormous body around, change direction at will, and tear himself free and charge away gleefully.

I could have sworn that as he ran off there was a grin on his face! The addition of side-reins and a longeing cavesson helped contain his playfulness and get this jovial giant under control again. It is, however, exactly this playfulness that has made it easy for him to learn; the rider can use this characteristic to her advantage while training. Every new exercise is a welcome challenge for the prankster-type horse (provided the rider does not use force).

This type of horse needs variety, both within each training session and over the course of the week. Turnout, free-jumping, trail riding, and "silly" games or tricks all help to keep the prankster willing and interested in ridden work. The rider will get much enjoyment out of this kind of horse, but should be forewarned that if she tries to suppress his lively tendencies, it will eventually become uncontainable and may result in behavior problems.

The prankster should be handled sternly but with understanding, both in-hand and under saddle. Ample vocal praise, pats and strokes, and treats work miracles, but limits must also be set and upheld. If you give the horse an inch, he will gladly take a mile. Once a prankster has had the opportunity to dominate a person, he becomes difficult to handle.

Remember, the prankster likes to be inspired—much more than his other four-legged friends. Thus the basic levels of the Training Scale (rhythm, suppleness and relaxation, and contact) are of the utmost importance, because it is this foundation that determines whether the horse will work *with* or *against* the rider, and whether future training will be fun for all involved, or a fight.

THE OVERACHIEVER

This type of horse is characterized by his enormous work ethic and a high degree of ambition, which is sometimes falsely interpreted as nervousness. The overachieving horse wants to learn and to please. He frequently anticipates, meaning that he acts ahead of his rider's aids, and therefore makes mistakes. It can be difficult to get this type of horse to relax, often due to the rider's inappropriate reaction to her horse's anticipation.

The owner of an overachieving horse should count herself lucky. She must only learn to steer her horse's ambition so that the horse doesn't "get in his own way." When this is achieved, working with this type of horse is a pleasure.

Common Training Mistakes

It is fundamentally wrong to punish the horse for mistakes that result from his eagerness to learn and to perform. In addition, frequent repetitions of the same exercises should be avoided.

This mare is always very enthusiastic about her work, and because of her eagerness to please, she can become quite hot.

PACE YOURSELF

In the case of the overachiever, the rider often has to set limits. This type of horse will try his heart out, even with new and difficult exercises. Because of this, it can't be forgotten that often the horse must develop a certain degree of physical conditioning and strength for many movements, whether in or out of the dressage arena. Just because an overeager four-year-old reacts beautifully to sideways driving aids, does not mean that he is ready to school half-passes. And if a young, athletically gifted horse offers a "swingy" trot, full of impulsion, and almost passage-like steps, it does not mean that he has developed the high degree of carrying capacity required to actually school the passage. If the rider wants to enjoy her horse for many years, she must restrain herself from practicing everything that the overachiever offers of his own accord.

Training Tips

So, you have an overachiever? Congratulations! As previously stated, it is not the overachieving nature of the horse that causes problems, but the way in which the rider reacts to his eagerness. If you can learn to keep this type of horse happy, you can teach him *anything*. In the dressage ring, it is the overachieving horse that is said to be "electric," meaning he reacts immediately to subtle aids, is sensitive to the leg, has a healthy desire to go forward, and is willing to learn. It is also this type of horse—assuming he has good jumping ability—that can complete a technically difficult course better than others. A famous example of such a horse is Shutterfly, ridden by Meredith Michaels-Beerbaum. Those that have an overachiever should cultivate this personality trait as the gift that it is, instead of trying to stamp it out. This begins with basic training and continues on throughout the horse's daily life.

Once rhythm, suppleness and relaxation, and contact have been achieved (or even, more simply, just "gas, brakes, and steering"), it is a good idea to teach this type of horse simple dressage movements in order to utilize his mental capacity and keep him from getting bored.

With overachievers it is important to take many breaks during a work session, allowing the horse to "chew the reins out of the rider's hands" and relax. This helps the horse learn to wait for the rider's aids rather than anticipate.

Note that it is important not to endlessly repeat the same exercise. The best example in the lower level range is the simple change of lead. While a rider of a slow, stolid horse can repeat this exercise 10 times in a row, an overachiever should only be asked two to three times in succession. Once he realizes what is coming next, he no longer waits for the rider's aids—he anticipates. This will only make the simple change worse: the horse will likely jig rather than walk in between canter leads and he will become tense. The more the rider tries to practice the now-not-so-good simple change in order to improve it, the more stressed the horse will become, since he now feels the rider is holding him back—he understands he is supposed to pick up the new canter lead, but he doesn't "get" that he is supposed to execute pure walk steps in between departs. When the rider continues to practice the movement and perhaps now punishes the horse for "misbehaving," the horse becomes even more tense and exasperated. This vicious cycle takes the joy out of the work for this naturally willing animal.

Instead of repetition, the rider should make a point of adding variety within a movement. Ride two simple changes, then ask for something completely different, and then eventually ask for one or two more simple changes. If the horse still doesn't wait for the rider's aids and execute a correct simple change of lead with clear walk steps in between, then the rider must increase the number of walk steps for training purposes. Instead of requiring three to four steps, the rider can have the horse walk for 10 or more. Or, she can ask for a leg-yield or shoulder-in (for more advanced horses) at the walk, which helps prevent the horse from predicting what comes next. The horse must wait for the rider's aids—exactly what he is *supposed* to learn—and while waiting, he relaxes. As you now know, relaxation is a prerequisite for successfully performing any movement.

The same rule described above holds true with more advanced overachieving horses during work on flying changes. The rider should avoid repetition of this movement so that the horse does not begin to change leads before the rider's aids, leading to possible mis-

CORRECT FEEDING PRACTICES

For generations, horsemen have known that horses can "feel their oats"—meaning they can become overly energetic and fresh from too much grain. Grains high in protein also increase the risk of colic and laminitis, and can lead to muscle stiffness and thus reluctance to work under saddle. But without grain at all (and without sufficient water and roughage), a horse does not have the nutritional reserves necessary for strenuous physical activity. It is important to find the correct balance of roughage, protein, fat, vitamins, minerals, and trace elements for your horse. The appropriate amount is influenced by the horse's work load, age, breed, size, and type. Most horses fall under the categories "light" to "medium-heavy" work. "Heavy work" is reserved for competitive racehorses or event horses in full training.

takes if done during the wrong moment in the canter stride. When a mistake does occur, the rider must not punish the horse. Instead, he should calmly ride a downward transition and ask for the original canter lead again. Then, at a suitable place he can ask for the flying change.

Even when no flying change was desired but the horse changed on his own—say, when riding counter-canter—it is important that the rider react calmly and without anger. This is especially important in the phase where the overeager horse is first learning the flying changes. Remember, this type of horse does not switch leads because he loses his balance or because he doesn't want to work hard in the counter-canter, but rather because he is proud to have learned something new and wants to demonstrate his prowess to the rider. If the rider punishes him in this situation, the horse will be completely confused. As a result relaxation will suffer, and with it rhythm and contact. This is the beginning of bigger problems, and with this sensitive type of horse can lead to serious training issues.

When an unwanted change of lead occurs as described, the rider is better off calmly acting as if he had asked for the change. He should canter a few strides and then ride a downward transition and canter off again on the desired lead. This way (and the same theory applies to riding all movements on an overachiever) the horse's eagerness can be channeled in a manageable direction.

The alert expression of a highly sensitive horse.

THE SENSITIVE HORSE

For the right rider, this type of horse can be a true gift. Sensitive horses usually have a healthy degree of forwardness, react well to light and subtle aids, and are usually obedient in a concerted effort to do everything right.

That is one side of the coin. On the other side they are quick to take offense at anything and everything they don't understand. This could be an incorrect aid, or simply one that was given too strongly or not clearly enough. Asking for a movement in the wrong place, such as a flying change too deep in the corner or a rein-back too close to the arena wall or fence, can upset a sensitive horse. As can minor equipment problems, such as a poorly fastened noseband. While many horses would not let such things ruin their composure, a sensitive horse definitely will. Therefore, this type of horse is only suitable for an experienced, skilled rider with a good amount of "feel."

Common Training Mistakes

It is a mistake for a rider with limited ability to ride a sensitive horse. Such a combination frequently ends in disaster, since this type of horse becomes easily insecure and frustrated by inappropriate aids or poor riding. Anger and punishment is inappropriate in the training of a sensitive horse.

Training Tips

Sensitive horses are best compared with artists or perhaps even geniuses. Their sensitivity is their strength and also their weakness. They can achieve great things but can also be inordinately upset by something miniscule and therefore stand in their own way.

The rider of a sensitive horse should see this character type as a gift and try to maintain the horse's sensitivity, including accommodating the horse's quirks. When the rider knows his horse well he will know what causes him stress and should deal with related situations gracefully, without becoming frustrated and angry. When a sensitive horse is trained in accordance with the Training Scale (see p. 17), his sensitivity is put to good use, allowing him to come "on the aids" and attain "throughness" (see p. 19). This type of horse will react to the most subtle of aids and the rider need expend little energy to ride him. When training problems (inevitably) occur along the way, the rider must be careful not to go overboard and use too much whip or spur, or to push the horse too fast. The sensitive horse reacts very negatively to harsh punishment or being pushed before he is ready, and such things can affect the horse's willingness to work in the future.

ISABELL WERTH AND SATCHMO

"The differences among the various horses that I have been able to ride over the years are one of the main things that make riding so fascinating for me. For example, when I think of Satchmo, I never

Isabell Werth experienced many ups and downs with the sensitive Satchmo.

cease to be amazed at how one can experience so many highs and lows with the same horse.

"By nature Satchie loves to move. I have never once seen him tired; his motor is always running. However he isn't 'hot' in the usual sense. He is very enthusiastic and can be a little overeager. In such instances I have to slow him down—not his forwardness but his eagerness.

"Even though many people won't believe it when I say this, Satchie is actually *not* spooky. Quite the opposite—he was, and still is, one of my best trail horses. Because of this I found it out of character for him when he frequently lost his nerve and had panic attacks during dressage tests. We tried everything for him: more work, less work, daily turnout, longeing, hand-walking, playing around with him, and he was repeatedly examined by the vets. Finally the vet found something while examining his eyes. Satchie had so called 'eye floaters,' meaning that he had an imperfection in his eye membrane that made it look to him as though something was quickly 'flitting' back and forth in front of him. This could very well make him panic. He had a successful eye operation that resulted in a definite improvement in his behavior. Gradually, he panicked less and less and began to remain calm even in the strange environment of a horse show.

"Working with Satchie is fun *every* day. At this point, our main focus is on gymnasticizing since Satchie knows all the movements already. He learned all the movements very quickly and easily since nothing was physically hard for him.

"To keep him happy, I also take him out on our galloping track. Or, I ride him over to my sister's farm and invite myself for a cup of coffee. Satchie is amused by the barking dogs and the gravel crunching underfoot and stands quietly next to me until I have finished chatting. This is mentally relaxing for him, and sometimes he doesn't even want to leave."

TYPES "MADE" BY THE RIDER

THE LAZY HORSE

The "lazy" horse is not a "natural" type—meaning lazy horses aren't born. Neither are "hard-working," horses, if you want to get down to it. The term "lazy" was designed by people to describe *people*. Laziness was considered one of the seven deadly sins in classical mythology. (Something that certainly does not apply to horses.) Rather, a horse is made "lazy" by his rider.

You often hear riders complaining, "My horse is so lazy!" but what they are interpreting as laziness is more accurately described as a horse that is "behind the leg aids" (see also p. 30). This can be caused by many factors. Feeding too little grain for the horse's workload can cause him to appear lazy, although really his "battery" has not been charged with energy. Certain health issues can also have an impact. For example, breathing or lung problems can deny the horse's muscles of necessary oxygen—you can check this through a blood-oxygen analysis. General nutritional deficiencies can be diagnosed with a blood test, and orthopedic problems, such as back pain or navicular disease, can be identified with X-rays.

However, the most common cause of so-called laziness under saddle is unfortunately rider error. An unbalanced rider with position flaws—such as a rocking upper body; stiff hips that don't follow the horse's movement; or a habit of landing heavily on the horse's back—combined with unclear and ineffective aids, can rob any horse (not just a slow, stolid one, see p. 29) of his natural desire to move forward.

The long-term use of rough aids, such as hard hands and overuse of the whip, as well as mentally or physically pushing the horse too fast or too far, can break his will, and out of a previously happy and forward horse a dull, reticent shell of his former self will remain.

Lazy horses often have trouble with rhythm, especially in walk and canter. The walk can quickly deteriorate into a pace and the three beats of the canter can become four. What appears from the outside to be relaxation in these horses is often not real relaxation at all. Their back muscles are often tight and cramped, and they carry themselves crookedly. Impulsion and collection are not attainable when the horse moves like this.

Common Training Mistakes

It is ineffective to attempt to drive an apparently lazy horse forward with incessant leg aids and constant use of the whip.

When the rider's seat follows the horse's movement, the horse can enjoy going forward, as exhibited by this pair.

Training Tips

Finding the cause of laziness is the first step. Once nutritional and health issues are ruled out, the rider must begin to analyze herself to see if she is causing her horse to be "behind the leg." An effective way of checking this is to let a very experienced rider sit on the horse a few times and observe what happens. Many horses respond right away by going forward when the rider's hips correctly follow and allow for forward motion. Other horses need a good rider to use two or three firm, well-timed aids as a reminder to move forward. However, the occasional "tune-up" is not enough to keep the horse forward in the long-term. It will not last if the horse's usual rider does not correct her position problems.

Unfortunately, it is especially hard for the rider to sit in a relaxed manner and give effective aids on a horse that does not go willingly forward. The more behind the leg the horse is, the more difficult it will be for the rider to correct her seat. Instead the rider will likely tense up her muscles in an effort to drive the horse, and acquire an unsteady leg that "nags" at her horse's side, making him even duller to the leg aids. Becoming dependant on longer and sharper spurs only adds to the vicious cycle.

A correct, fluid seat is a prerequisite for productive work on the elements of the Training Scale. The best way to improve a rider's seat

---

HEALTH CHECK

Character, conformation, gender, and breed all contribute to making each horse an individual. There is one very important additional factor: the horse's health. All too often horses are labeled resistant, stubborn, lazy, overly nervous, or unrideable when a health issue is the hidden cause. Teeth problems (sharp points or infection), lung problems, tight muscles or muscle disorders, metabolic disorders, and "kissing spine" are just a few of the health issues that commonly lead to riding problems. It is important for horses to have a regular checkup, as well as an additional examination if a serious issue under saddle suddenly arises.

International dressage rider Heike Kemmer demonstrates an unmounted exercise that can help improve rider position (right). Mounted exercises target specific aspects of the rider's position (left).

is through gymnasticizing exercises that target specific areas of the body. If possible the rider should work on her position with the help of a riding instructor, ideally on a horse that willingly goes forward. Then her new knowledge can be applied to the horse labeled "lazy."

Even the experienced rider that acquires a lazy horse must take certain actions. Certainly the most important is to look into the cause of the laziness. Is the horse behind the leg due to previous rider error, or has his joy of movement been robbed from him due to coarse, rough riding?

It is not so difficult to improve the first scenario. The rider must only give clear forward aids in combination with exercises that increase the horse's forwardness, such as riding transitions "forward and back." Riding in two-point position in the ring, as well as on trails, and including jumping gymnastics will help loosen the horse's muscles, rekindle his desire to move forward, and help achieve "throughness." Probable rhythm disturbances will also be improved with this work.

The second case is different and more complex. Horses that have been tyrannized with years of coarse and incorrect riding either become psychologically unstable and act aggressively, unpredictably, or nervously, or they become withdrawn, apathetic, and appear to have given up. About 30 years ago such a horse, a tall bay gelding, came into my hands. He had been trained through FEI level, and had competed through Third Level. At the time I was very inexperienced and didn't think twice about his blank gaze and the hairless sores where spurs had long prodded his sides. The gelding turned out to be extremely behind the leg, apathetic, and introverted. He would stand in the corner of his stall with his head lowered, as if nothing in his surroundings interested him. Although he could perform all the dressage movements, riding him was not fun as he had zero desire to do what he was doing. With the experience I have today I might have been able to help him (and myself), but at the time I was at a loss as to what to do.

This short, sad story is not meant to discourage riders, but to demonstrate how coarse riding can drastically damage a horse's psyche. You must always remember that sometimes your plans for your horse do not align at all with what the horse is suitable for.

THE FEARFUL HORSE

Fearful horses lack, above all, self-confidence. They are either born without it or they lose the little they have as they grow and are trained. Horses with a natural tendency toward fearfulness usually become even more fearful over time. In a herd, they are at the lower end of the hierarchy, and their fear is reinforced when other herd members bully them. Acquired fearfulness is due to environmental influences such as improper and abusive handling by people. When a horse that already has a fearful tendency is treated roughly, the combination can create a frequently panicked and possibly unrideable horse. Whatever the cause, a fearful horse struggles with all aspects of the Training Scale, especially—of course—suppleness and relaxation.

Achieving an inner calm, an important part of the element of relaxation on the Training Scale, is by nature very difficult for a fearful horse. Tension, spookiness, and shying, as well as a tendency to run away, make it very difficult for the rider to maintain a steady connection—a soft and trusting contact between the rider's and the horse's mouth. Fearful horses are only suitable for experienced and patient horsemen, and those who aren't looking for quick success.

Fearful horses tend to shy and spook, whatever the situation.

This horse plants his hooves in front of a supposed danger (the puddle), and looks skeptically behind him, displaying a combination of fearfulness and resistance. In such a situation the rider must react calmly but firmly.

Common Training Mistakes

The worst thing the rider can do is to react to a horse's fear by punishing him. The horse then connects punishment with the situation he is afraid of, which only reinforces his fear. The next time a similar scenario arises, the horse will not only be afraid of the object or situation but also of the punishment—and therefore, his rider.

This connection between fear and punishment occurs in all types of horses, but for the fearful horse it plays an especially strong role. On the other hand, it is also ineffective to try to soothe the horse through "babying." An overzealous, "Whoa, boy! Calm down..." can confuse the horse further instead of giving him security.

Training Tips

The rider must keep in mind that his horse's fear-based reactions are not directed toward him but are in his horse's nature and can be increased through negative experiences. Overly fearful reactions can occur at any time: while handling the horse on the ground or while riding him, and on the trail as well as while jumping or working in the dressage ring. Since both the horse's fear response and the "trigger" of the fear can vary, an experienced and sensitive rider is required to respond correctly, maintain control, and keep calm. One horse may be terrified of loud noises; the next is afraid of flapping objects; the next won't step on his own shadow; and the last is thrown into a panic if the rider gives an incorrect rein aid. One horse may always suck back and ball up, while another will jump sideways and try to run away from the danger.

As a rider of a fearful horse, you must remember that even though the horse's reaction may be exaggerated, he is still expressing his nature as a prey animal. Becoming annoyed or enraged will not improve the situation. Instead, building trust is the key to success. The chances of success and the methods for achieving it depend entirely on the nature of the horse's fearfulness.

Inborn Fearfulness

Inborn fearfulness is difficult for the rider to deal with because it is the horse's true character tendency (as opposed to *learned fearfulness*—see p. 65). Whereas the rider of a horse with learned fearfulness can replace the horse's memory of bad experiences with good experiences, the rider of an innately fearful horse must turn a "cowardly chicken" into a "brave lion"—something that cannot always be accomplished.

The rider must keep in mind that a truly fearful horse has been that way since birth and has acted according to that fear since his first days under saddle, probably as a three-year-old. Such a horse hasn't *lost* his self-confidence; he *never had any* to begin with. His mother probably didn't encourage self-confidence in her offspring, likely because she was also a fearful horse and imprinted this behavior on her foal during his most formative period. He can't turn to other herd members for confidence-building, either, since he is low-rank and bullied. Nor can a horse be helped with the kinds of therapy a human with fear issues might consider.

However, an experienced horseperson can, within limits, help an innately fearful horse gain confidence. Patience, creativity, "feel," and the "right touch" are necessary. For example, specific groundwork exercises can help the horse learn to focus and engage with people. Another possibility is using relaxation techniques, such as Linda Tellington-Jones' TTouch bodywork (www.tellingtonttouch.com). Introducing a friendly and steady companion to the fearful horse, either in the pasture, or while riding in the ring or on the trail, can work wonders. The second horse sets an appropriate example for your mount to follow. And most importantly, the horse's handler must behave calmly and rationally at all times so the horse learns to trust her and look to her for reassurance.

Linda Tellington-Jones uses her unique Tellington TTouch system of bodywork to help fearful horses relax.

Learned Fearfulness

In the case of *learned fearfulness*, humans have instilled fear in the horse. This problem can be easier to deal with than innate fearfulness (see p. 63), but not always. The challenge is for the rider or handler to regain the horse's trust. As a first step, the handler must try to figure out what kind of negative experiences the horse has had and what exactly he is afraid of. Is he afraid of a person's hands? A whip? Specific movements when being ridden? Certain aids from the rider? Or does pretty much everything to do with people inspire panic? Once the source of the horse's fear is identified, the handler can begin to address situations in which the horse has previously had negative experiences, and replace the horse's bad memories with good ones.

For example, if a horse was taught to rein-back using too much force on the reins, or was beaten when he didn't back up correctly, or if rein-back was used as punishment for other mistakes, this movement will be associated with trauma. The worse the horse's experience, the more frightened he will be of the rein-back and eventually of being ridden and of people in general.

To teach the horse to work in a relaxed and fearless way, he must first be handled calmly on a daily basis, and then the fear-inducing exercise (in this case, the rein-back) can be gradually reintroduced in a casual or fun manner, with and without a rider. Vocal praise and treats should be used as positive reinforcement.

When reintroducing an exercise, the handler or rider must try to prevent the situation from becoming stressful for the horse. Should the horse panic, the handler should try to ignore it. When dealing with a problem with rein-back, if the horse takes so much as a single tiny step backward, regardless of how it looks or if you really wanted three or four steps, praise him amply. Try to be satisfied with very little. The process of regaining the horse's trust can take days, weeks, or even months. But it will, although at first almost imperceptibly, begin to change the horse's behavior so that he slowly becomes more engaged and less fearful.

When I write about the fearful horse, I speak from experience. Many years ago, my second horse (after graduating from ponies) was a 14-year-old Trakehner gelding that was trained (to a certain degree) to FEI level and was supposed to "teach me" upper level dressage movements. What we didn't know was that the horse was notorious in our area for being "crazy." Truthfully, he wasn't crazy; he was only afraid—completely and utterly afraid of the rider. I will admit that at first I cursed the day that I was advised to get involved with him. But as fearful as the gelding was, he was also lovable. He was gentle, observant, and a little shy, and he—despite everything—craved human affection.

Working with this gelding was a challenge. He was so fearful and nervous that on some days he was nearly unrideable. However, we managed to qualify for the German Junior Championships (the competition still existed in those days) and even managed to be in the top seven placings the first two days. The third day was a nightmare—a

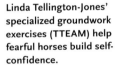

Linda Tellington-Jones' specialized groundwork exercises (TTEAM) help fearful horses build self-confidence.

DON'T CODDLE THE FEARFUL HORSE

Fearful horses should be ridden and handled calmly and cautiously. However, the rider must not coddle the horse by trying to keep him away from the realities of the outside world. Hiding the horse away "in a bubble" is, first of all, not really possible, and second will not help the horse conquer his fears. When the horse is only ridden alone, in the same arena, where all noises are kept to a minimum, dogs are prevented from running around, and rustling plastic bags are carefully removed, then the horse never learns to deal with his fears and trust his rider. Outside factors are important and shouldn't be kept away. Of course, the introduction to "scary" situations is best done a little at a time: the process should be gradual and as soon as the horse reacts calmly, he should be praised.

score of "4" was our highest mark in our dressage test. My horse couldn't help it; he was simply finally overcome by panic.

When we returned home, there was lots of talk about how it was no surprise: the gelding had already gone through many hands because he was so difficult. So difficult, in fact, his former owner had two riders warm him up at horse shows. The first would ride for an hour; then the next would ride for an hour. Their "aids" must have been severe; my horse had deep scarred grooves on his lips in the corners of his mouth. It was logical that this horse eventually began to associate being ridden with "being tortured."

You couldn't hold a whip anywhere near him, whether on the ground or mounted. He was terrified of the rein aids. An accidental movement with the hand or a slightly too strong aid would set him into a panic and induce a reflex of repeatedly jerking his head in the air. The horse would then become more upset as the rider's hands would (inevitably, in such a situation) not react perfectly. To address this problem I decided to longe him with side-reins. On the longe he still threw his head frantically, but the side-reins provided him with a constant, steady connection from the bit to the girth, and he gradually began to trust the rein contact and his fear of the rider's hand diminished.

When a horse fully trusts his rider, you can perform what would otherwise be considered fright-inducing tasks, such as opening an umbrella in the saddle, as I have done here on La Picolina.

The success I had on the longe line inspired me to try riding him with side-reins, as well—regardless of the fact that (on a good day) we were at Third Level or that many people scoffed at and gossiped about this strange method. To make a long story short, our weekly training regimen consisted of three days in a row of longing, then two days of relaxed riding in side-reins, followed by competition on the weekend. Gradually, out of the "crazy" Trakehner, a reliable and successful dressage horse emerged. He learned to trust the rein contact and his mouth healed. He could be ridden with or without a whip. He eventually took me to my first placings at FEI level, and he would follow me anywhere—all without fear.

Of course, this doesn't mean that every horse that suffers from learned fearfulness just needs side-reins and your problems will be solved. It does demonstrate, however, that with such horses, even an unorthodox method can lead to the end goal, as long as the method is appropriate for the needs of the individual horse. Each horse's needs

Long, long ago: My Trakehner (although admittedly short in the neck) and I walk calmly forward during an awards ceremony.

can be as varied as the causes and sources of his fear, and the rider must be prepared to search for a unique solution.

THE RESISTANT HORSE

The resistant horse is another type that is not born but rather develops for various reasons. Such a horse vehemently resists (more or less) everything that his rider asks of him. The resistance can take the form of head tossing, bolting, bucking, kicking out, rearing, "climbing the arena walls"—or even throwing himself against them! Depending upon the severity of the resistance, the horse should not be in the hands of an inexperienced rider, and even an experienced rider must understand the risks involved in dealing with such a horse.

KLAUS BALKENHOL, GRACIOSO, AND GOLDSTERN

"Over the years I have dealt with all possible types of horses. The most unique horse was definitely Gracioso—and his character was the complete opposite of my famous mount Goldstern's.

"When Gracioso first came to me he was very fearful and intro-verted. He recoiled and withdrew equally from strange people and objects, and often bordered on out-of-control. Because he was so skeptical and overly sensitive, he was quick to become tense and had problems under saddle with rhythm in trot and canter.

"In order for me to further his training he had to learn to trust me. My first goal was to make him less fearful, to accustom him to people, and to make him a little more approachable. I went into his stall many times each day simply to give him treats and pet him. At first he would stand with his head facing the wall, but gradually he began to turn expectantly toward me. He slowly began to open himself up under saddle as well. My wife, Judith, and my daughter, Anabel, rode him as well. Their job was to focus less on his training and more on relaxation, so that he learned not to fear his riders and that work under saddle did not always mean hard work but could also be fun and laid back. The more he relaxed the more rideable he became, and his talents began to present themselves. I think that even today, I don't know of a horse with such an exceptional piaffe and passage. He always remained a bit of a shrinking violet—the complete opposite of Goldstern, who also cost me a few sleepless nights, but for different reasons.

"Goldi was a combination of a prankster (p. 44) and a hot horse

Gracioso was a fearful horse...

...whereas Goldstern was a hot, prankster type (see pp. 34 and 44).

(p. 34). He loved to move and was always outgoing and friendly toward people. He had a strong personality and a tendency toward dominance, possibly because he was gelded late. He wanted to assert his position as a horse and in the process always created a positive challenge for his rider.

"In order to manage his hotness, which was especially predominant in his youth, we used Linda Tellington-Jones' relaxation techniques (www.tellingtonttouch.com). Of course, Goldi was also worked in accordance with the classical principles of the Training Scale, with variety in his work schedule, and we allowed time for him 'to just be a horse' as much as possible. Improving his relaxation, although we continuously had to work on it, allowed him to excel in his dressage career.

"Although they were each so different, Gracioso and Goldstern constitute real proof that trust and relaxation play a central role in training a horse."

Common Training Mistakes

It is wrong to react with force and violence without understanding the cause of the horse's resistance.

Training Tips

General resistance in a horse usually has a story behind it. It can have to do with sickness, or injury, or bad riding, or a combination of these things. Many riders immediately reach for harsher bits, sharper spurs, draw reins, and other brutal "teaching tools" before looking for the cause of the behavior. Analyzing the answers to a few questions first can usually shed some light on the problem.

Did the resistance suddenly occur in an otherwise rideable and well behaved horse? If the answer to this question is "Yes," then the fit of the saddle and bridle should be checked. If these fit and are adjusted properly, then a veterinary checkup is the next step.

What form does the resistance take? Does the horse react by suddenly tossing his head, is he extremely hard to bend in one direction, or oversensitive to rein-aids? This can be a sign of a tooth problem such as sharp points or infection. Does the resistance consist of sudden stopping, and bucking or rearing? Does it disappear on the longe, without the weight of the rider? This could be caused by kissing spines, a very painful irritation of the spinal process.

If the difficulties under saddle have slowly developed it could be a combination of a health issue and rider error. For instance, increasing laziness in the horse can be a result of ineffective aids from the rider (see p. 56) or of a slowly developing illness, such as a lung problem or an orthopedic issue (for example, navicular disease or osteoarthritis).

When a resistance problem occurs over time, the rider must look to herself to see if her riding techniques could be the cause. For example, while an increase in shying can be the result of a progressive eye problem, it can also be due to timid and ineffective riding. The better the rider knows her horse and the more she knows about riding in general, the sooner she will be able to pinpoint the source of resistance and solve it.

It is only in very rare cases that a horse, possibly due to an inability to be friendly toward people and a difficult character, will engage

Such resistant behavior presents a danger to both rider and horse.

in resistance just for the sake of it. And it is only in these exceptionally rare instances that for the safety of both man and horse, drastic measures are warranted. However, if the slightest doubt exists that perhaps a hidden health issue or rider error could be the underlying cause of the resistance then, for the horse's sake, the problem must be further investigated.

SPECIAL CASE: THE YOUNG HORSE

The young horse is not a type in the traditional sense. It is a category that is defined by a time period in which specific characteristics are exhibited. The inexperience of the young horse is paired with his natural character and often presents itself as curiosity or uncertainty; high spirits or slowness to learn or catch on; meekness or dominance; and more or less constant growth.

Young horses are not yet well educated under saddle and cannot be asked to do very much. Thus, they are not suitable for inexperienced riders. Nonetheless, one often hears relatively new riders (after three to four years of riding, I'm afraid you are still considered

Bucking and kicking out can be caused by pain, but can also be a sign of a struggle for dominance.

"new" to riding) saying, "I'll buy myself a young, unspoiled horse—a 'blank slate'—so that we can learn together." The idea is nice but is not realistic. No one would advocate for you to try to teach someone else a foreign language when you can't yet speak it yourself; or, having heard of the theory of relativity once or twice, try to explain it in detail to another. It always works best, whether in a language class, physics, or riding, to learn from someone with experience in the subject. In riding this means not only to learn from an educated riding instructor but also an experienced horse.

Common Training Mistakes

As I've already mentioned, it is unwise for an inexperienced rider to take on a young horse. Other common mistakes include treating a young horse like an older horse (expecting him to behave like his more mature counterparts) and pushing a young horse too fast.

Training Tips

Riders with limited experience and ability should purchase an older, well-trained mount. Three- or four-year-olds should be absolutely off limits, regardless of how pretty, good, sweet, or well-behaved they seem. Six years old is a minimum age and 10 is ideal—by then, horses are calmer and less likely to become easily upset or nervous. If they have a reasonable amount of training for their age, they will by this point have a clear understanding of the aids, so that even a rider in the process of learning will be able to communicate, to some extent, with the horse.

Riders that already have a young horse should be clear about the typical characteristics of this age group. It is quite normal for young horses to be high-spirited and this behavior is not something you should attempt to eradicate. If young horses are forced to behave within narrow parameters, you risk taking all joy out of their riding experience, and with it their "spark." On the other hand, the rider must not allow all poor behavior to continue, as simple "good spirits" can quickly become naughtiness and dominance. Even recognizing this fine distinction requires much experience, "feel," and ability.

Young horses can be overtaxed all too easily. In the first two or three months after the horse is started under saddle, it is a good idea

Young horses, like this one, can be high-spirited and reactive. Inexperienced riders would likely be quickly overwhelmed in such a situation.

to ride him only two or three times a week for about 20 minutes, tops (see more about this on p. 77). The rest of the time, in addition to daily turnout, the horse should be longed. Once he has slowly built up his strength and found his balance under the rider, the sessions can be gradually increased until they occur daily.

A young horse lacks condition and training, meaning that both his muscles and focus are quick to tire. Strength and concentration capacity take time to build up. Experts say that a horse can only really focus for 20 minutes at a time, and a young horse for an even shorter period. Thus, regular walk breaks are crucial while riding. If frequent breaks are not taken, the horse's physical and mental relaxation will diminish.

Working with a young horse requires attention to the Training Scale (see p. 17). When the principles of the Training Scale are not fully understood by the individual in charge of the horse's training, you might hear a frustrated comment like, "My four-year-old picks up his head and looks around at the halt, so I'm getting out my draw reins," or, "He wasn't 'through' at all today." Of course a four-year-old will sometimes lift his head and look around. He is not yet secure with the contact, is still curious and unfocused, and is usually more interested in his surroundings than his work—not unlike a child in kindergarten. If a four-year-old wants to take a quick peek around at the halt, then he should be allowed. Becoming irritated or punishing him for this will only make him insecure.

As contact improves and the horse becomes older and more mature, these issues will resolve themselves. You cannot talk of "throughness" in a youngster—at best "rideability" or "un-rideability" must suffice. Rideability is an inborn characteristic, whereas "throughness" is the goal as well as the result of correct training in accordance with the Training Scale. "Throughness" calls for mastery of the elements of impulsion, straightness, and collection.

Once they have found their balance and strength, most young horses—depending on their character—will sooner or later test their rider and even attempt to throw her off. This is normal and is no reason for quick and rash actions. Grabbing for draw reins, beating the horse, or becoming overly afraid of the horse are all inappropriate responses. Further work and training is the solution. And remember, a little bit of friskiness should be allowed, but limits must be set. This way, the horse learns that ridden work requires concentration but is also fun and challenging.

Another important factor to consider when working with young horses is their growth patterns. Stallions grow until they are four or five years old. Mares grow up to age six or seven. During this time not only does the horse's height increase but his joints mature and fuse. This affects his balance and carrying capacity.

The horse's body can change over a course of days or weeks, which of course has a constant impact on the balance that he has just worked so hard to find under his rider. Some horses grow "evenly," meaning that the height of the forehand and hindquarters remain level and harmonious throughout their growth period. With other

youngsters, and especially with those destined to be tall, the withers and croup seem to take turns growing, so sometimes the croup is much higher. It is possible for there to be a short period where his body is relatively level, and at this time he can easily find rhythm and present himself as rideable. Then, a few weeks later after another growth spurt, difficulties reemerge that had been seemingly resolved. This process can drag on until the horse is three or four! The rider must recognize this and adjust his work accordingly. Sometimes taking a step back and patiently practicing the most basic exercises is necessary.

"Büffel" as a five-year-old (left) and at six (right). It is easy to see here how much a horse develops over the course of a year when in steady training.

Even with horses that grow evenly or those that have nearly finished growing, ridden work must be appropriate for their age. Although three- or four-year-old horses sometimes look or act like older horses, appearances are deceiving. They are neither mentally nor muscularly mature. Their tendons and ligaments are not as strong as those in older, more trained horses, and even their bones and joints are still developing. The same is true for growing children, whose long-term health can be damaged by hard physical training at a young age.

Overwork of a young horse not only occurs through too long and overly intensive work sessions but also through inappropriate selection of movements and method of exercise. For example, riding a high number of extensions at the trot should be avoided since this puts a heavy strain on the horse's tendons. Lateral movements—especially the half-pass—shouldn't be practiced too early or too often while the joints are still unstable and not fused.

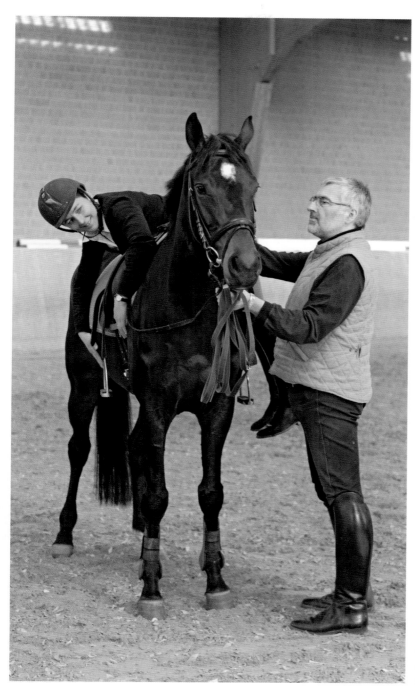

Young horses should be started under saddle by experienced riders.

Isabell Werth and Warum Nicht FRH.

RIDING ACCORDING TO CONFORMATION

Until now the horse types that I have discussed have dealt with the horse's character (what's "inside"). Now I will address common types of the horse's "outside" or build and appearance, also known as conformation. As with character types, each conformational type necessitates a different emphasis while riding and training. Depending whether a horse is equipped with a very short back; a very long back; a steep or a well angled hindquarter; a high- or low-set tail; a heavily muscled under-neck; or another defining physical characteristic, the rider may have to change his training approach (although still adhering to the Training Scale) and possibly alter his goals. Because the horse's anatomy is unchangeable, certain conformational deficiencies can hinder the horse's progress and limit his abilities—especially when several conformational weaknesses are present at the same time.

Big and small, long and short: Every horse is unique in appearance and build.

THE SHORT-COUPLED HORSE

Very short-backed, or "square," horses have the advantage of a strong back that can carry weight well. However, they also have a tendency to hold their back tensely and lack the desirable "swing" through it. When the horse can't "swing" through his back, his general movement has a "stuck" quality—his muscles aren't supple and loose. As a result physical relaxation suffers, and then mental relaxation diminishes, as well.

The short-coupled horse's carrying capacity is often quite good but his "pushing power" leaves something to be desired, which in turn limits his development of impulsion. Short-backed horses that do manage to generate good pushing power tend to track wide behind in trot extensions. Moving sideways is usually easy, but true bend from poll to tail (also within lateral movements) is a challenge due to reduced flexibility of the spine.

Common Training Mistakes

Many riders are fooled by the short-backed horse's apparent ability to collect and do not devote enough attention to lengthening and suppling the horse's neck and back muscles.

This Warmblood has a rather short back for his breed.

Lateral movements such as shoulder-in, shown here, are important for suppling a short-backed horse.

Training Tips

Short-backed horses can be any breed, commonly Baroque horses, such as Andalusians, and Quarter Horses, which have been intentionally bred with short backs to help them serve an intended purpose. The muscular difficulties that arise in short-backed horses are the same in all breeds, regardless of whether the horse is a Baroque horse, a Western horse, or a jumper. When working with this type, even if only for reasons of keeping the horse healthy, special emphasis should be placed on stretching in order to relax the muscles.

A useful tool for these horses is riding and or longeing over trot poles and cavalletti. This requires the horse to lengthen his neck and stretch his frame forward and downward, which not only positively affects his back but his hindquarters, as well. Thus, a short horse is made longer, and as the back and neck muscles are stretched the horse's movement is better able to swing through his whole body.

A very useful way of improving the horse's ability to stretch forward and downward is riding lateral movements. At first leg-yield can be used, and for more advanced horses shoulder-in, travers (haunches-in), and renvers (haunches-out) are helpful. Short-coupled horses should be especially well gymnasticized to avoid further shortening (and therefore tension) in their muscles.

Another recommendation is to let the horse stretch while cantering out on the trail or on a galloping track. (Attempting to stretch forward and down at an extended trot is not as helpful for two reasons: Firstly, riding repeated trot lengthenings is strenuous for the tendons and joints, and secondly, short-coupled horses tend to become quick rather than truly lengthening their stride, which leads to muscle tension rather than stretching.) In an energetic, forward canter, the

TROT POLES ON A CIRCLE

When riding trot poles on a circle, the distances between the poles can be easily varied by angling them: When the horse trots on a smaller diameter circle, the poles lie closer together, and when trotting on a larger sized circle, the poles are spread further apart (this causes the horse to stretch more). Alternating smoothly between more stretching on the larger circle and more bend on the smaller circle increases the horse's suppleness and ability to "swing" over his back.

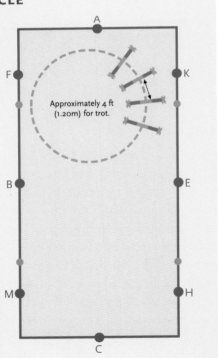

Approximately 4 ft (1.20m) for trot.

horse must stretch and use his whole body to maintain a consistent rhythm. It is important that the rider allows the horse to stretch and doesn't restrict him with his hands. A short-backed horse that is worked in this manner will be better able to maintain the desirable "swing" through his body during collection.

Another key factor with this type of horse is the careful selection of a saddle. On a short-backed horse, there is—of course—not very much room for a saddle. When the saddle is positioned to allow for the necessary freedom of the horse's shoulders, the panels of certain saddle designs extend too far back over the horse's kidneys. In this case the assistance of an experienced saddle fitter is crucial.

Short-coupled horses must be encouraged to stretch forward and down. Here, the horse's nose could reach outward slightly more.

HUBERTUS SCHMIDT: RIDING ACCORDING TO CONFORMATION

Hubertus Schmidt and Wansuela Suerte.

"During my riding career I have had a number of extremely different horses to ride. Long-backed horses, short-backed horses, croup-high horses, geldings, mares—really everything. In my experience, it isn't as important how the horse is built, but primarily whether or not the horse's conformation—ideal or not—will allow him to do dressage. And the next factor is whether the horse is, by nature, willing to cooperate.

"At one point a gelding came to my stable. He was extremely long-backed and somewhat croup-high. When I first saw him without a saddle on, I was shocked and asked myself, 'How can this horse do advanced dressage movements?' To my great surprise, the gelding had a wonderful piaffe and passage, despite the fact that his conformation did not at all predestine him for this. He didn't let his imperfect body get in the way of his willingness to work. We must let go of the notion that a horse must have perfect conformation; what is important is whether the horse can work with the conformation he has.

"The rider should try to identify the horse's strengths and weaknesses and use gymnasticizing exercises to improve areas in need. For example, I ride a hot horse (p. 34) a little under tempo and implement many curved lines and rounded figures, whereas I will send a slow, stolid horse (p. 29) freshly forward. A short-backed horse tends to move more upward than forward, so I will work him in a deeper frame.

"On the whole, when training a horse, the rider must do the opposite of what the horse tends to overdo by himself."

THE LONG-BACKED HORSE

The long-backed horse is often jokingly called a "family horse" because there is room enough on his back for the whole family to ride him at once. This funny idea aside, long-backed horses present serious challenges for the rider. The "bridge" between the forehand and the hindquarters is long, and therefore sensitive, so these horses often have difficulty carrying weight. "Pushing power" and carrying capacity are often limited, as is the horse's ability for collection. Long horses also struggle with the elements of rhythm and straightness. While long horses are often capable of more movement along their spine, this can lead to muscle and ligament damage if they are ridden incorrectly.

When the silhouette of the short-backed horse from p. 84 is laid over the photo of the long horse, it is easy to recognize the difference between them.

Common Training Mistakes

Long horses tend to let their hind legs trail out behind them, thus letting their back drop, instead of stepping well under their center of gravity. If this problem is not addressed the long horse will become increasingly strung out, which negatively affects the back, the joints in the legs, the muscles, and "throughness." Riding with draw reins only exacerbates the problem.

This Warmblood mare has a rather long back.

A typical problem with a long-backed horse: the rider uses too much hand to shorten the horse, causing the back to drop and the hind legs to trail out behind the horse's body.

Training Tips

When working with a long-backed horse the emphasis should be on the hind legs. The hind legs are the motor that must be activated so that the horse can step under the rider's weight, and (at least optically) shorten himself. This shortening of the frame must apply to the whole horse, from back to front. This means that the neck and poll can only come in toward the horse's body (by becoming rounder) as much as the hind legs step under the body. Although draw reins are very popular with this type of horse, they are not beneficial, since they only shorten the front of the horse and thereby further block the hind legs from stepping under and the back from "swinging." This only promotes the problem of trailing hind legs. Long-backed horses that are ridden with draw reins on a regular basis are usually short in the neck but even "longer" behind the saddle.

When the horse is trained classically, the back lifts and the hind feet step deep under the horse's torso so that his whole body becomes "shorter." To accomplish this, many half-halts are necessary. With

Much improved: The rider has softened his rein aids and increased his driving leg, allowing the mare to step further under her center of gravity and lift her back, especially in the lumbar area. The horse appears slightly shorter behind the saddle than in the previous picture.

younger horses, half-halts are mostly used in preparation for new movements and downward transitions. With older horses they are used for changing the pace within a gait—for example, the rider asks the collected horse to collect even more for a few strides before resuming normal collection.

Of course half-halts are immensely important for every horse and the quality of transitions shows how well the horse is ridden. For the long-backed horse, half-halts are the key to success. A rider on a horse with ideal conformation may give 15 half-halts in a two-minute time span (a general estimation, although the number depends on the horse's age, training, and the movement being ridden) whereas a rider on a long horse should give 30, at least.

Riding transitions is beneficial for all horses since it combines gymnasticizing with strength-training for the hindquarters. In every transition the hindquarters should sink down a little, even if it can hardly be seen, and the joints in the hind legs must bend and compress more. This is especially difficult for long-backed horses; during half-halts and transitions they sometimes try to make their job easier by balancing on the rider's hands. In this event, the rider must respond instantly with an appropriate rein aid and a driving leg (see p. 32 for more on the driving leg). The rein aid should not be confused with pulling on the reins. If the rider pulls the horse will only lean harder or pull back. Instead, even while half-halting, the rider's hand must remain flexible and "play" with the connection to horse's mouth. It is a balancing act: The rider must keep the horse's neck and poll in the desired position, but must also be quick to soften and give so the horse never has a chance to lean on the reins.

In addition to many half-halts, riding soft bending lines is helpful, although very challenging for long horses. Long horses tend to let their hindquarters swing to the outside in turns, like those trucks with the signs that read "Caution, wide turns." To prevent this habit,

A long horse working at a very collected canter. The horse has been asked to spiral in from a larger circle onto a smaller circle and the rider is asking for a travers (haunches-in). An assistant can help and provide guidance with a whip, as I am here, but note that this is a fine-tuned aid and nothing more.

the rider must consciously use her inside leg to keep the
horse bent and to drive the horse into her outside rein. At the same
time the rider's outside leg needs to keep the horse's hindquarters
on track. If the horse is consistently ridden this way in turns and
corners he will be obligated to take more weight on his inside hind.
Over time, this will strengthen his hindquarters, helping him step
under his center of gravity more easily and allowing him to appear
shorter-coupled.

There have been many examples of long horses that have reached
the top levels of dressage compeition. For example, the famous chestnut mare, Wansuela Suerte, did not have ideal conformation but was
nonetheless brought to the Olympic level by Hubertus Schmidt (see
p. 88).

After strenuous collected
work, long horses must be
allowed to relax by stretching
forward and downward. In
this photo, you can see the
hind legs are clearly stepping
further under the horse's body
than at the beginning of the
day's work session (see photo
on p. 90).

THE CROUP-HIGH HORSE

It is generally difficult for a croup-high horse to become a dressage horse. The aim of dressage training is to improve and perfect collection, which requires a lowering of the croup. The haunches are supposed to take on more weight and lower slightly while the joints of the hind legs bend more significantly. If the hindquarters are already higher than the horse's forehand, it is twice as difficult to lower them (especially if the hind legs are also quite straight). The rider should keep in mind that a croup-high horse must work against his own conformation to accomplish the goals of the Training Scale.

The croup-high horse can be prone to developing problems in the sacroiliac joint and the stifle.

Common Training Mistakes

Ignoring this particular conformation flaw can have negative effects on the horse's "throughness," athletic capabilities, and health. Inappropriate gymnastic exercises can be just as harmful as attempting to force the horse's hindquarters to lower artificially.

Since she was a foal, La Picolina's croup has been somewhat higher than her withers (this page, and top right). Through work appropriate to her build and stage of training, this fault didn't hinder her development as a dressage horse (bottom right).

Training Tips

It is perfectly normal for a horse to be croup-high while he is still growing (see p. 74). The forehand and hindquarters often alternate growing so that at one point the croup will be higher than the withers, and then the height of the withers will again overtake the hindquarters. If the horse's hindquarters are higher than the withers when the horse has finished growing, usually between ages five and seven, then the term "croup-high" can be applied. When searching for a dressage horse it is not necessarily ideal to choose such a horse. However, owners of croup-high horses should not despair! You simply need to take some points into consideration.

Horses that are extremely croup-high should not be pushed into a serious dressage career. By doing so the owner puts his horse under a lot of pressure. A horse with a willing attitude will try his hardest but will eventually be limited by his conformation. And a less willing horse will resist the work from the beginning, simply because it is too difficult—or even impossible—for his body to accomplish. Neither scenario is very appealing. A technically skilled and physically strong rider can sometimes "squeeze the horse together" so that he can perform surprisingly advanced movements, but this is only due to the expense of great physical force on the rider's part and results in wear and tear on the horse.

This conformation is not nearly as problematic when the horse is only slightly croup-high. Nonetheless, there are things to keep in mind when working with such a horse. Like the long-backed horse, the croup-high horse should be stretched forward and down to strengthen and lift the back. Horses that are slightly croup-high have a tendency to develop a swayback with age (see p. 120). This can be very subtle at first, but with improper work it will become more noticeable. The leverage effect produced by the back's shape can also lead to problems with the stifle in the sacroiliac joint. If the rider succeeds in strengthening and lifting the horse's back through gymnasticizing and conditioning (using half-halts, transitions, and school figures), then the horse can maintain an athletic outline, despite being croup-high.

My Grand Prix horse La Picolina, called "Liese," is an example of a croup-high horse.

When riding La Picolina, I must keep her hind legs active and stepping under her body.

She's a three-quarter Thoroughbred, but has a rather flat wither (unlike the breed typically demonstrates). However, like many Thoroughbreds, she is slightly croup-high. Due to her enormous willingness to work and friendly nature, combined with good rideability, intelligence, and otherwise correct conformation, she is easy and fun to ride. I do have to focus on activating her hind legs, though. If this is neglected, "Liese" won't step under her body as much as she could. This is not because she is lazy or negligent but simply because of her conformation.

THE VERY TALL HORSE

The height of a horse depends, among other things on the standard size range of his breed. In comparison to years ago, Warmbloods are now a little taller, so as to better fulfill the various sport purposes they serve. A height between 16.2 and 16.3 hands is completely normal, although both smaller and larger horses are not uncommon. Isabell Werth's Apache measures 17.3 hands and Warum Nicht FRH is 18 hands (see p. 104). While there is nothing particular to consider when working with smaller horses (except that they should be an appropriate size for their rider) very tall horses do need special consideration.

A tall horse like "Büffel"—17.3 hands high—must be given time to learn to sort out his long, gangly parts.

Most XXL-horses are "late bloomers," meaning that they need more time to develop than smaller horses of their age. The bigger the horse, the bigger everything will be, including the movement. Riding an uphill, ground-covering medium canter on a large green horse in a 20- by 40-meter dressage ring is challenging and will leave quite an impression. And small, tight turns in a jumping course can also be difficult for the tall horse and his rider.

Especially tall horses like "Büffel" usually need a longer warm-up phase before beginning a workout.

With a very tall horse there should be extra emphasis placed on improving his rideability; and increasing his bend, "pushing," and carrying power, and his "throughness." If this is neglected then the imposing, tall horse can quickly become an inelegant "mack truck."

Common Training Mistakes

Riders of tall horses should not resort to stronger equipment (draw reins, harsher bits, double bridles) in place of proper riding in order to "shorten" and gain control of the horse. Failing to gymnasticize a tall horse as he should be is also a mistake.

Training Tips

With extremely tall horses—those measuring 17 hands or more—not only is the horse's movement bigger, but so are all of his "parts." Long legs, long neck, long back—this additional "mass" must be activated and cultivated. Young, tall horses need more time to find their balance under saddle. A growing tall horse is like a growing youth basketball player whose gangly extremities appear not to belong to the rest of his body. Once the horse has developed and matured so his conformation is harmonious from nose to tail, he will be better able to find his balance and synchronicity of movement if trained correctly.

Riding school figures such as circles, voltes, and serpentines are beneficial for tall horses.

Unlike basketball players, the tall horse's height has disadvantages as well as advantages. The tall horse must perform the same movements in the same size ring as his much smaller opponents. Voltes, serpentines, changes of direction through the circle, and zig-zag half-passes are all movements that improve a horse's "throughness," but they are much more difficult for a tall horse to complete. The rider of a tall horse must keep this in mind at all times. This does not mean the rider should assume these figures are too difficult for his horse and never ride them—then the horse will never become more supple and balanced. But if the rider demands too many or too small figures from the horse, the horse will be overwhelmed and possibly become resistant (see p. 69). For instance, the rider should at first ask for a 10-meter volte rather than a 6-meter, and ride only three serpentines instead of four. When turning up the centerline the rider should begin the movement a little early so the horse has room to make a wider turn.

The rider must give fine-tuned half-halts to help the extra-tall horse attain self-carriage and "throughness."

Riding changes of pace in the canter, as well as frequent voltes and circles, improves the tall horse's carrying capacity without the use of strength by the rider.

Tall horses often need a longer warm-up phase than smaller horses. They are more like a truck than a sports car: They are equipped with a lot of power but right after starting up the engine, they need a little time to warm up. Only then can they begin to complete more demanding maneuvers. It is as though it takes a few moments longer for impulses in the hind hooves to travel through the horse's long legs, over the back, and to the brain—and vice versa.

After riding at the walk during the warm-up, the rider should progress to the trot. Cantering right away is not ideal for the tall horse as it is more taxing for the muscles. Since bigger horses inevitably have more muscle mass than smaller ones, the rider should be careful that her "mountain of muscle" has the time to stretch before asking too much of him.

When an average-sized horse realizes that he is stronger than the rider, difficulties quickly arise. These problems can usually be solved by skillful technical riding. However, when a 17.3-hand Warmblood realizes his strength...you might be in trouble! The bigger the horse, the more he needs to be made responsive to subtle leg and rein aids. Rounded figures (voltes and circles—although not too many or too small), half-halts, halt transitions, rein-back, and lateral work are especially beneficial training exercises for large horses, even more so than for smaller ones. The rider must be very careful with the strength of her aids. Although strong aids occasionally become necessary, the rider should keep them to an absolute minimum. Otherwise she runs the risk of dealing with a strong opponent rather than a powerful partner. When that occurs, riding a big horse is no longer enjoyable—it is just work.

ISABELL WERTH AND WARUM NICHT FRH

"'Hannes' (Warum Nicht FRH) is a completely different type of horse than Satchmo (see p. 54). The one thing they have in common is their shared desire to 'go forward.' But that is the only thing. At 18 hands, Hannes is quite a giant, and exemplifies all the characteristics that one would expect from such a big horse. On the ground he is a prankster, self-confident, cheeky (not to mention colossal). But under saddle he is timid. This of course makes him very unique. He reacts with fear to anything that is 'under him' on the ground. Sometimes I think this has to do with his height and his extremely long legs. Maybe he worries that in a dangerous situation he won't be able to coordinate his legs quickly enough to get away! As a young horse he would get really upset, and even now he will hesitate if something unusual appears on the ground. It doesn't help to kick him or try to force him past it; he will only close himself off to the rider and become extremely strong. I have learned instead to take three deep breaths and to relax myself, in order to help him relax.

"Hannes" during a dressage test...

"For a time we put flowers and chairs around the arena and hung up blankets and other objects along the fence. Once we even laid a carpet on the ground in front of Hannes' stall door. (At big indoor shows the horses sometimes have to walk over carpets to enter the ring.) It took a lot of effort to get him over that carpet—we shook grain in his feed bucket, and even though he was hungry, at

first he still completely refused to get near it. We carried on
with this desensitizing for about a year until he was used to everything we could think of. Now and then we still put a few flower
pots in the ring while we work so that he doesn't forget the courage
he's acquired.

"There are other challenges under saddle due to Hannes' height.
Of all the horses that I train, he is the one that I most often ride low
and deep. I focus on many, many transitions when working him.
When you look at his conformation, you see a long-lined horse with
long legs, a long neck, and a big body. Everything fits harmoniously
together, but he has to sort out all his big parts. Hannes also needed
an extra year—as compared to my smaller horses—for his muscles to
develop and mature. These are all things that one must take into account when working with such a big horse. While Hannes was quick
to learn the technical aspects of the dressage movements, his skill at
performing them with expression developed over years."

...and training at home.

POORLY CONFORMED LEGS

Toed-in, toed-out, cow-hocked, bowlegged—there are many conformational problems of the legs or hooves that over time can lead to joint issues such as degenerative arthritis, and have a negative or limiting effect on a horse's rideability. When choosing a horse, pay close attention to conformational faults in the legs. For owners of horses that have such issues, it is important to be cognizant of their possible impact on your horse's health and performance.

Common Training Mistakes

It is irresponsible to ignore the possible negative effects of a horse's leg conformation and to push him down a certain career path despite these faults.

Training Tips

The owner of a horse with faulty leg conformation should discuss the issue with the horse's veterinarian and farrier. While they can't work miracles and turn crooked legs into straight ones, the experts can minimize negative effects of the problem(s).

Corrective shoeing (like insoles for people) can be very helpful, but must be done gradually over time. If the horse's legs are abruptly straightened or a high wedge is suddenly added to one side of a hoof, the horse may very well go lame.

The rider should discuss with the veterinarian which under-saddle exercises may be beneficial or detrimental to the horse's legs. For example, a severely bowlegged horse (with hocks set wide apart) should not work for long periods in extreme collection or repeatedly perform lateral movements. The increased bending and sideways rotation of the hocks during these exercises puts more strain on his body due to this conformation flaw than a they do on a horse with correct hocks.

Practicing exercises for too long or too often that are not suitable for the horse's conformation will lead to the horse tiring quickly, being generally overtaxed and possibly becoming resistant (see p. 69). If the rider is not in tune to the problem and punishes the horse when he cannot complete an exercise correctly, then a psychological problem is added to a physical one.

This doesn't mean that horses with flawed leg conformation should not receive dressage training. Basic dressage training and gymnasticizing in accordance with the Training Scale (see p. 17) and appropriate to their conformation is both beneficial and healthy for these horses. The situation is similar to a person who has one leg that is slightly shorter than the other. If the person is outfitted with an insole or a lift in his shoe, then he can exercise like anybody else in order to gain physical fitness. And so it is that when a horse with mild leg faults gains overall muscle strength from exercise, he is far better off than if he doesn't exercise at all. It is the rider's responsibility to recognize the extent to which her horse's deficiency can be compensated by training while also identifying the limit of her horse's athletic capabilities. If the horse is pushed past this point, the rider is placing an irresponsible strain on her horse's health.

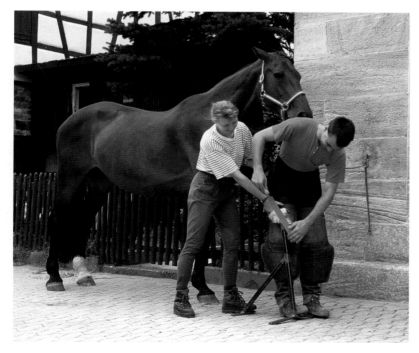

Corrective shoeing can improve issues due to faulty leg conformation.

THE DIFFICULT NECK

The length and shape of a horse's neck can indicate possible problems in his rideability and give insight as to how he should be ridden. The way a horse's neck is set not only has aesthetic impact, it also affects the activity of the back. The horse's head, neck, and rump are connected by three muscles: the *longissimus cervicis*, the *spinalis thoracis et cervicis* and the *semispinalis capitis*. Together these muscles support the nuchal ligament, which allows the horse's back to be raised without muscle engagement when the horse lowers his head and neck.

This system functions best in a correctly shaped neck: neither too long nor too short, slightly rounded and tapering gradually from the shoulder to the poll. When the horse is worked correctly, the upper muscles in a well-shaped neck are quick to develop. But, even an ideal neck can be "mis-developed" through incorrect riding, so that the under-neck muscles protrude.

A neck with strong under-muscling loses much of its ability to lift the back via the nuchal ligament. This becomes even more difficult when the neck is also too short or too long (it should relate harmoni-

A   A correctly shaped neck.

B   A neck with overdeveloped muscling underneath.

Haflingers have somewhat short necks. This mare carries herself with her forehead in the ideal position—in front of the vertical—but the muscling on the underside of her neck is braced too prominently.

ously to the rest of the horse's body); does not taper as it approaches the poll; or is set too low at the shoulder—such as a ewe neck (upside-down neck—see p. 115) or if it has an exaggerated, unnatural curve like a swan (see p. 114).

Common Training Mistakes

When purchasing a horse, the shape and development of his neck should not be ignored. If your horse has a difficult neck, attempting to deal with it via hand-riding and the rein aids alone will not be successful.

Training Tips

Of course the neck must be considered in conjunction with the rest of the horse. A horse with a slightly problematic neck but otherwise good conformation can still be highly rideable and develop well with proper training. Nonetheless there are a few basic approaches that are helpful when considering specific neck issues.

The Short Neck

Horses with relatively short necks often have difficulty with contact and connection. They frequently hold their head behind the vertical. When asked to bring their nose more in front of the vertical, they tend to lift their head higher and brace with the muscles on the underside of the neck. When this happens, they are no longer "through" at the poll or moving "over their back." The rider should respond by encouraging the horse to stretch forward and downward into a soft contact with the bit. This is done as with the long-backed horse (see p. 89), by riding half-halts and transitions. The horse will respond to a correct half-halt by rounding his neck slightly and seeking contact with the bit.

With a horses that becomes "locked" at the poll rather than letting

A Through bending exercises such as shoulder-in (shown here with slightly too much angle toward the inside of the arena)...

B ...and with repeated half-halts, this mare's short neck appears to lengthen.

his poll and neck fall forward and down in a relaxed manner, it is very helpful to ride rounded figures, such as voltes and figure eights, as well as shoulder-in and travers (haunches-in). As the rider applies the inside leg during these bending exercises, the horse is encouraged to "give" at the poll, let his neck fall, and stretch into the contact. While the short neck cannot actually be made longer, through this kind of work it appears and functions as if it were slightly longer because it departs from the shoulder at a different angle.

Trot poles and cavalletti (see p. 86) are excellent tools for encouraging a horse to stretch. To test that horse and rider are on the right track, the rider should ask the horse to stretch and the horse should maintain his steady tempo and rhythm while reaching forward and downward to seek contact with the bit.

The best way to test that your gymnasticizing work is correct is by asking the horse to stretch forward and downward, as this mare is here.

The Long Neck

In itself a long neck is not problematic. On the positive side, it offers enough room for muscle to develop. However, if correct muscling is not continuously built up, a long neck can become a very difficult neck to manage.

At the end of the neck hangs the horse's very heavy head (45–65 pounds/20–30 kilos, on average), which is supposed to be "carried" by the nuchal ligament (see p. 108). A horse with a long, thin, under-muscled neck will try to support the weight of his head by leaning on the reins. He will either curl his neck up with his chin against his chest or tip his forehead and engage the muscles surrounding the 3rd or 4th vertebra (a "broken" neckline) instead of keeping the poll as the highest point.

In both cases the contact is incorrect and it is difficult to rees-tablish a true connection. This has various negative effects, includ-ing the fact that the back is not able to lift properly, and transitions, which are so important in daily training, cannot be performed smoothly.

For these reasons a long neck should be carefully strengthened so that it can perform its job correctly. The neck should be first strengthened with stretching work (forward and down—see p. 111). Without stretching, muscles cannot build strength properly. Then gradually the neck can be raised from the stretching position; at first only for short periods before returning to stretching, and later for longer.

It is important that as the rider gives a half-halt she does not pull with a stiff hand, as this gives the horse something to lean against. Instead she must soften her hand at the moment when the horse begins to carry himself, even if the horse can only maintain self-car-riage for a few seconds. In the moment of self-carriage, the upper neck muscles engage, especially where they meet the upper edge of the shoulder blade, and gradually become stronger so that over time, the horse collects himself more easily. The long neck becomes some-what wider at its base so that it is better equipped to carry the horse's heavy head while maintaining the poll as the highest point. And, if the rider has soft and light hands, the horse will learn that he doesn't need the support of the reins because he can carry himself.

The muscling of the horse's neck can be checked by the rider while in the saddle. The rein contact should be very light so the horse has the freedom to carry his head as if there were no rider aboard. The neck should ideally be slightly wider or equally as wide on the end closer to the withers as it is on the end closer to the head. If this is the case then the horse's training has strengthened the correct muscles. If instead, the neck is narrower at the end near the withers than at the poll, or widest around the 3rd and 4th vertebrae, then something is wrong. In this case, in order to prevent further problems, you must return to the basics, stretch the horse forward and downward, and ride many, many, transitions. Patience is required because an incorrectly developed neck cannot be fixed in a few days. Rebuilding the muscles is required—which can take weeks to months—before moving on with training can be considered.

A **Correct:** The strongest muscles are in the horse's upper neck along the crest—indicated by the blue.

B **Incorrect:** The upper-neck muscles are not developed, but the muscles on the underside of the neck and around the 3rd and 4th vertebrae are overdeveloped (indicated by the red).

C **Incorrect:** Underdeveloped upper-neck muscles and overdeveloped muscles on the underside of the neck.

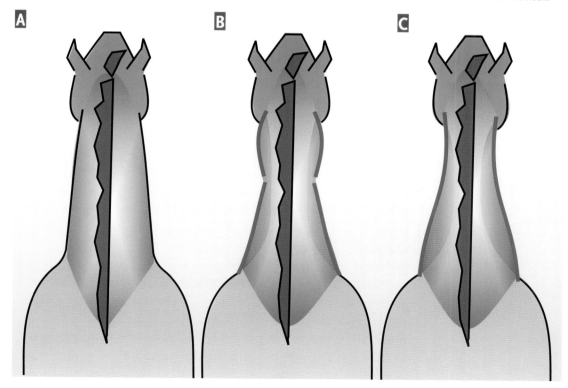

The "Swan Neck"

This neck conformation is generally found on horses with long necks. While a swan neck is considered a conformational flaw in some breeds, such as Warmbloods, in others (Arabians, Orlov Trotters, and Friesians, to name a few) it is a desirable trait. The swan neck is usually set on very high and encompasses all the disadvantages of the very long neck (see p. 112). In addition, depending on the shape of the neck, horses with this trait tend to have problems with contact—for example, high-headedness or head-tossing (often seen in Arabs) or "crunching" their neck in like an accordion (a common problem in Friesians). When training a horse with a swan neck, special emphasis should be placed on the element of contact from the Training Scale. Stretching the horse forward and downward should play a central role in the horse's daily work so that he learns to let his neck "fall" (see p. 85). Where applicable, do not forget that this conformation is bred into the horse and therefore cannot be completely changed by your riding.

The Ewe Neck

As the name implies, this neck conformation is shaped like that of a sheep: set on low and featuring prominent muscling on the underside of the neck. For those who ride dressage, this is certainly the most difficult neck conformation to deal with, and it is hard or impossible to improve. Ewe-necked horses usually struggle with basic rideability. They have a hard time balancing under the rider's weight since stretching forward and downward is difficult for them, and thus so is lifting their back. This can lead to problems with rhythm and maintaining a consistent contact, and eventually results in tension, which rules out the desired relaxation.

Since it is very difficult—even for a rider with optimal aids and ideal coordination of the leg, hand, and core—to convince a ewe-necked horse to stretch, auxiliary reins are helpful in this situation. Vienna reins are an effective choice, as they limit the upward reach of the horse's head while allowing and encouraging him to stretch forward and downward.

If the horse gives and softens his topline in the Vienna reins, the rider can begin to add more half-halts and figures into the training program. Only when the horse can complete circles and voltes with the Vienna reins hanging slack is it time to try schooling without them. At first they should be removed toward the end of the training session, and each day they should be taken off a little sooner so the horse spends progressively more time without them.

If the ewe-necked horse is worked very correctly with a focus on lifting his back, then his bad neck can be changed a little. The muscles under the neck can be slightly diminished and the muscles on top of the neck can be built up, even so much so the neck will eventually almost resemble a normal neck. However, the fundamental anatomy of the neck cannot be changed, and the problems will persist, although they can be somewhat mitigated.

When riding a horse with a ewe-neck, "throughness"—which is the essence of the Training Scale (see p. 17)—must be a focal point, even more so than with other conformational types. To accomplish this it helps to ride the ewe-necked horse in a deeper frame than horses with other neck conformations.

The "Knife Neck"

A "knife neck" is one that lacks the ideal rounded muscling along the crest. In profile the horse should have a softly rounded topline, but a horse with a knife neck has a very straight (think "sharp") outline from the withers to the poll. Horses can be born with this neck shape, or it can develop with incorrect riding. It is generally harder for horses with this trait to "give" and be supple at the poll. As a result, all elements of the Training Scale are affected, especially rhythm and contact.

If the horse is carefully and correctly gymnasticized, the upper neck muscles can be strengthened and the shape of the neck will improve. Note that it does take more time than it would with a correctly shaped neck. However, if the rider puts the horse in a fixed frame with the reins, so that the horse's head is at the vertical but the horse is not actually working from back to front and supple at the poll, then the knife-neck conformation will persist and ultimately strengthening of the hindquarters will be neglected.

Even if my classical-riding readers shake their head in dismay,
I advocate riding a knife-necked horse a little deeper and rounder
than other horses, even if he comes slightly behind the vertical in the
process. Why? It's simple: A horse with this trait—whether inborn
or developed over time (the conformation fault can develop when the
horse is never ridden "through"—see p. 19)—has difficulty rounding his neck. Instead, the horse finagles his neck position so that the
only thing that happens is his head is brought down. At first glance,
the horse appears to be on the bit, as the poll is in fact the highest
point. But to accomplish this, the horse shortens his upper neck
muscles, and the withers do not lift, the back doesn't "swing" (it stays
stiff and tense), and the movement doesn't carry through the horse's
body. The goal is for the horse to round his neck and become accus-
tomed to carrying his neck in this shape, whether it is positioned low
or high. Only then can the nuchal ligament do its job and raise the
horse's back.

A typical "knife neck": The neck is not poorly set on the horse's body but note the "sharp" straight line along the crest and overdeveloped muscles on the underside of his neck.

The more often this type of horse is ridden deep, the more his upper-neck muscles can stretch and therefore strengthen. When a knife-necked horse is warmed up and stretched in this manner, he will also have better inter- and intramuscular coordination and less "inner friction," meaning the muscles can produce more power—power that the horse can use in his neck to carry his head as gracefully as possible and to lift his back.

If despite gymnasticizing work, the horse still will not "give" at the poll and round his neck, and health issues related to the neck and back vertebrae have been ruled out, then side-reins—correctly adjusted and implemented—can be helpful.

Correctly adjusted side-reins (neither too long nor too short) will help this type of horse learn to round his neck. Vienna reins (which I've recommended in other instances, see p. 115) are not an ideal choice for knife-necked horses as they give the horse the option of simply extending his head out and down without rounding it. Draw reins are also not well suited to training this type of horse. They allow him to hang on the reins instead of encouraging him to round his neck and carry himself.

When using side-reins under saddle, ride the same gymnasticizing exercises that you would ride without them: half-halts, transitions, circles, and voltes—all the exercises that improve "throughness" and help keep the horse on the aids. Over the course of the ride the side-reins should hang slack, which will happen if—as previously mentioned (see p. 117)—the horse is allowed to be slightly behind the vertical. When the horse is sufficiently warmed up, the rider will have no problem bringing his nose in front of the vertical with an appropriate half-halt.

To gauge the appropriate length for side-reins used under saddle, the rider stands in front of the horse and gently pulls his head forward. The horse's head should be able to reach to the vertical or only slightly in front of it.

SWAYBACK AND ROACH BACK

Both of these conformation flaws can be problematic since the back is the center of the horse's movement. A swayback is a back that dips down (lordosis) and has a diminished weight-bearing capacity. A roach back (kyphosis) is a back with an unnatural upward bow just before the croup. It is less flexible than a normal back.

True lordosis and kyphosis are inborn and uncommon conformational flaws. But dips or upward bows in a horse's back can be caused by other factors. Broodmares often develop swaybacks over the years. Their back muscles are not highly developed since they are usually not in work, and the weight of their belly at advanced stages of pregnancy eventually pulls their poorly supported vertebrae downward. Tendons and ligaments wear out and the back sags over time—so age is a common cause. A horse that has a weak back by nature can develop a swayback from incorrect riding.

A roach back can also be the result of incorrect riding, but unlike the inborn roach back, the problem lies in the soft tissue rather than the bones. If the rider relies on strength or draw reins to pull her horse together, she can cause the horse to move with a cramped, tight

This gelding has a slight swayback. It is not significant enough to be problematic, but nonetheless, an emphasis should be placed on lifting his back correctly during training.

Here the rider purposefully demonstrates incorrect riding for the photo: When the horse's neck is incorrectly elevated the hind legs lack impulsion and trail behind him. In this moment, the horse's back is clearly dropped. If this incorrect riding continues, the horse's swayback will worsen.

back, and the horse can develop a bulge of muscle behind the saddle that resembles a slight roach.

Both the swayback and roach back that are induced by incorrect riding negatively affect all elements of the Training Scale (see p. 17). They especially hinder the horse's movement from "flowing" from the hindquarters over a relaxed back, and thus make it very difficult for the rider to maintain a balanced seat, particularly in trot.

A With the assistance of Vienna reins the same horse is encouraged to let his neck fall and bring his back up. The hind legs step further under his body on both the straight lines...

B ...and on bending lines.

Common Training Mistakes

Ignoring back problems, such as a sway- or roach back caused by poor riding, and continuing to ride without changing style or technique is certainly the worst mistake the rider can make. It can lead to serious health problems in the horse.

Training Tips

If the horse's back has either sunken or formed a bulge of tight muscle behind the saddle due to incorrect riding, the rider must take several steps back and begin again with the horse's training as if he were young or green. The rider should include the following in the horse's work sessions: Riding at a forward tempo; rising to the trot; changes of pace (using half-halts); large rounded figures such as circles and figure eights; and increased stretching forward and downward. During this review work, Vienna reins may be used if necessary.

Following this elementary routine, the sagging back will gradually lift and the tight bulge of muscle in the "pseudo" roach back will loosen and eventually disappear. The corrective work can take weeks, months, or longer, depending upon the severity of the sway or roach. In addition to work under saddle, longeing (two to three times a

The same horse as on p. 121 after brief use of Vienna reins: There is a clear improvement in the lift of the back in trot and canter and the hind legs step well under his body.

week), jumping gymnastics (see pp. 33 and 38), and physical therapy are helpful.

WHEN CONFORMATION GOES ALL WRONG

It is sad, but true: There are horses with such bad conformation that almost no part of their body is correctly shaped. Perhaps one such individual has a big head, thick throatlatch, a ewe or swan neck, an upright shoulder, a long sway- or roach back, a short croup, and crooked legs—such a horse isn't suitable for athletic activities. At best he can be a trail horse (depending on his faults—see below), a companion horse, or a pet, assuming he is of a friendly nature.

Common Training Mistakes
Attempting to turn a horse with very bad conformation into a competitive athlete will only end in frustration for horse and rider.

Training Tips
Those with competition-oriented goals should steer clear of horses with very poor conformation. Depending on which conformation faults a horse has, he may even be ill-suited for pleasure riding on trails. For example, an improperly set neck can so negatively affect the horse's rideability that he becomes unsafe, even on a trail ride.

If you tell yourself, "Surely, the horse and I will work it out," your positive thinking is misplaced. There is no way to cure a combination of major conformational flaws. Even the best rider and the most willing horse have no chance in this situation.

Remember this, especially when considering a horse that is being sold cheaply or given away—if it is because of overall terrible conformation, it is not a good deal. Once home in the barn the horse's upkeep will be at least as much as other, less problematic horses. Plus, sooner or later he is likely to develop health issues caused by one or more of his conformational problems, which will further add to his cost.

GENDER TYPES

Britta Schöffmann and La Picolina.

GELDING, STALLION, OR MARE?

This question is posed by many who are searching for the ideal horse. And the answer must be carefully considered since the difference in character among the genders can be significant. Geldings are usually the least complicated, but of course, there are always exceptions to the rule. On the following pages I describe some of the typical differences you find when comparing the sexes.

GELDINGS

Since many gender-based character traits result from hormonal influences, geldings are less prone to related behavior and mood swings. Upon castration, the concentration of hormones in the horse's blood plasma and serum decrease significantly and remain at a very low level in comparison to that of stallions. Thus, the nature

Geldings are considered uncomplicated riding partners.

of a gelding is mainly influenced by his character rather than by his hormones. This leads to the statement I made earlier, that geldings are usually less complicated than mares and stallions.

Common Training Mistakes

There are actually no mistakes that are specific to handling geldings. However, geldings are frequently rumored to be less sensitive than mares and stallions. This is a misconception. Lack of sensitivity and stubbornness are character traits that are independent of and unrelated to gender and are instead usually innate or bred into the horse.

Training Tips

Since there are no specific problems, there are no specific solutions. In the event that difficulties arise when working with a gelding, the rider should look into training issues, character traits (see p. 22), conformation factors (see p. 82), or breed tendencies (see p. 140) for a possible cause.

STALLIONS

The typical stallion is, in many ways, the product of his hormones, if not their slave. Stallions tend to exhibit varying degrees of dominance and macho-behavior. This is not naughtiness or misbehavior; stallions are by nature intended to be dominant and assertive. Otherwise, they could not combat their opponents and pass their genes on to the next generation in the wild. This fact means that riders and handlers of domesticated stallions must be hyperaware of their character, habits, and preferences.

On the one hand, a stallion is always quite impressive with his powerful neck and imposing behavior under saddle and in-hand. On the other hand, it is exactly this power and behavior, combined with the horse's strong will, that can make daily handling of a stallion complex and even dangerous. It should be noted that stallions are generally not appropriate for the inexperienced!

With their imposing behavior, stallions can be unpredictable on the ground. It is a good idea for stallion handlers to be hyperaware of the horse and his actions.

Common Training Mistakes

When handling or riding a stallion it is just as wrong to be too lenient as it is to be too forceful and demanding. It is also wrong to mistake the horse's display of power under saddle for "collection." When you make this mistake, you allow the horse to build up more and more tension, and it may eventually be released in a dangerous manner.

Training Tips

Stallions have especially complex personalities, since they are not only influenced by their character and their conformation but also to a large degree by their hormones.

There are a few basic rules that should be observed. Most importantly, when working with stallions, situations where there must be a winner and a loser should be avoided whenever possible. This may sound complicated and theoretical, but it is actually simple. It describes a relationship between horse and rider in which there is a mutually respectful partnership. Now and then each has their chance to have the upper hand, but neither feels defeated. This rule actually applies to all horses, but stallions are especially likely to test their handlers. Remember, this is not due to nastiness on the horse's part; it is simply in his nature to challenge rank.

It is important, however, that unwanted behavior on the ground is not tolerated. For example: nibbling on the handler or her clothing; grabbing the reins or lead rope with the teeth; pulling while being led; dancing around; and taking exaggerated interest in other horses—these are all signs that the stallion is testing the people around him in order to at some point completely take over. If the handler lets herself become "second in command" on the ground, then she is bound to have problems under saddle.

To avoid this, strict but fair handling must be practiced everyday with a stallion. This means that depending on the stallion's character, undesirable behavior such as nibbling a jacket or chewing on reins should be discouraged with a quick slap with the hand. Dancing around can be disciplined with a sharp, meaningful pull on the lead shank. The punishment should never be brutal; it should be done calmly but with enough energy or strength to discourage the unwanted behavior. The same is true for work under saddle. Many stallions, even the most well-behaved and least problematic, tend to occasionally present dominant behavior. This can manifest as nickering while passing by other horses, small bucks, kicking out when touched by the rider's leg or whip, unwanted flying changes, and a whole host of other problems—big and small. These are a stallion's way of keeping his rider on her toes. If the rider allows such behavior to pass without consequence, the stallion will quickly take the upper hand and begin to up the ante until serious insubordination results.

KARIN REHBEIN AND DONNERHALL

"My best known stallion was definitely Donnerhall. He was really extraordinary and actually very sweet. That isn't necessarily true of the other stallions I have ridden over the years. When I can choose, I am more inclined to ride geldings or mares. A stallion tends to have a mind of his own and wants to have his own way. In order to progress with a stallion, the rider must maintain control from the start. If stallions are not a little bit subordinate, massive problems can occur.

"It is also especially difficult when stallions have an athletic career as well as a breeding career. There are not many stallions competing in dressage that have successfully combined the two. Donnerhall was one of them; he could recognize the difference between breeding and dressage work. Donnerhall came to us as a weanling and was completely uncomplicated from the beginning. He never questioned who the boss was. The only thing he ever did was occasionally kick out to the whip (which he absolutely hated). He was a drastically different horse from another stallion, Nektar, that I showed—he had to be castrated because his stallion behavior ruined every dressage test. Even Cappuchino can be distractible in the show ring.

Karin Rehbein and the unforgettable Donnerhall

"For a while, stallions were really fashionable, but that trend is over now. I personally believe that a stallion that is not licensed and doesn't breed would likely have a better life as a gelding, and also be easier to ride and handle."

STALLION FAD

For a time it was popular to have a stallion as a riding horse. Friesian and PRE fans were especially enthralled with this idea. Of course from a breeding standpoint, it is useful for stallions to be trained as sport horses. For the average pleasure rider one must ask if riding a gelding or a mare wouldn't make more sense. Even the best behaved stallion can end up in a situation where he tries to assert dominance, or his hormones can simply get the best of him. Anyone that deals with stallions on a regular basis should keep this in mind— for safety's sake.

While riding a stallion it is very important to discourage the smallest of disobediences and to punish the horse if necessary. For example, the horse should accept a subtle aid with the whip (and I mean "aid," not a "whollap") without a disobedient retort. If the horse reacts by angrily kicking out, the rider should respond with another touch with the whip. If necessary this can be repeated so that the rider, in the end, has the last word. As mentioned earlier, however, the rider must limit such "discussions" so that they never escalate into a battle. If it comes to this, the rider risks losing, even if it appears that she has won. How can this be? If the stallion wins the fight, he will no longer respect the authority of the rider and also not see her as a partner. This is an unpleasant and risky position for the rider to be in if she is to continue working with the stallion. If the stallion loses a fight there are two possible outcomes: either the stallion's spirit will be broken and he will lose his "spark," or he will become unpredictable and hateful toward humans. Both outcomes are a lose-lose situation.

Over the years I have worked with many different stallions including a very handsome and talented individual that I brought from a young horse up to wins at Intermediare II and placings at Grand Prix. "Maneken," as we called him, was always scheming up new ways to disobey in the back of his mind. Out of 10 competitions, he was unbeatable in eight, and in the other two he pulled all sorts of nonsense, including unwanted flying changes everywhere and other fresh behavior.

Our relationship was a good one—a combination of friendship and partnership. Occasionally we would have a confrontation but it never ended in a winner or loser. Everything went relatively well until I decided—with the correct training of my horse in mind and out of modesty for my own ability at the time—to bring Maneken to a "top trainer" so that he could help me with the fine points of our piaffe and passage. This professional training only lasted three weeks, but in this short time my brilliant charmer became a broken horse. The trainer, who had barely missed riding in the Olympics, answered every little bit of cheekiness from my stallion with a merciless show of force. In my youthful lack of self-confidence, I was too slow to question this "experienced" trainer's ruthless attitude. Once I was finally able to speak up and end the training arrangement, it was too late. At the slightest of leg aids the stallion would bite himself in the chest, and he would urinate at the lightest touch of the whip. It took a year before we regained our understanding. Sadly, the "spark" that this wonderful horse once had never returned. I am still riddled with guilt over the fact that I didn't disregard this trainer's "big name" and immediately take my horse away from him.

With stallions there is a very fine line between giving in too soon, logically but sternly following through, and forcibly overpowering the horse. Stallions require the rider to posses a high degree of technical skill and experience as well as a great deal of empathy and understanding of horses—more so than with mares and geldings.

Many stallions, like my handsome Maneken, are better off taught in a playful manner than with pressure and force.

JAN BRINK AND BRIAR

Jan Brink and Briar.

"Because of breeding, I train many stallions including the exceptional stallion, Briar. However, I will admit that geldings are generally the least complicated horses to work with. It is just my lot that I ride so many stallions.

"Stallions can be tricky, especially in the show ring. There are stallions that know exactly where the dressage test begins at 'X.' When compared to mares, I find stallions often easier to work with because they accept more straightforward aids. With mares the rider must make many more compromises. When on a stallion or gelding, the rider can give an aid, a signal, and the horse will usually immediately do what the rider asks. With a mare the rider must carefully formulate the aids—it is as if he must fill out a contract and ask for permission before the mare will agree to work with him.

"Regardless of the horse's gender, the rider must learn to listen to his horse. Stallions, to a greater degree than other horses, must not be pushed too hard or too fast. When this happens they quickly become dull to the aids and behind the leg, and their spirit fades. Today I know enough to use my 'head' to respond to a stallion's dominance issues rather than my physical strength or force. A stallion must be managed in a very specific way to keep him on the rider's side.

"For example, when Briar is not preparing for a show, he is simply conditioned rather than schooled daily. He already knows everything; it is pointless to have him practice it everyday. Instead he is ridden on the galloping track, on the trails, and is turned out in his paddock. He is often gymnasticized long and low in a snaffle. I am of the opinion that the rider should not overpractice that which the horse has already mastered. Piaffe can be ridden once or twice a week, and trot extensions should be ridden even less often, as they are strenuous work for the horse. Many riders make the mistake of practicing everything over and over again. When the horse does a movement well, the rider should stop working on it for that day rather than asking for the movement five more times until it gets worse instead of better. This will bore and frustrate any horse, not just stallions.

"If I ever feel that when working a horse I am in his 'stress zone,' I take a few steps back into his 'comfort zone.' The rider must keep in mind that nothing has to happen today, there is always a tomorrow."

A stallion that can regularly enjoy turnout will also be a happy riding horse.

It is important to provide stallions with as "natural" a life as possible, even though this is more difficult than with geldings or mares. Many stallion owners recoil at the thought of turning out their stallions. If a stallion is introduced to turnout at a young age, the facility is equipped with an extra high "stallion fence," and a compatible gelding can be used as a neighbor or pasturemate, most stallions can adjust successfully to it. Since stallions are very intelligent and thrive on variety, turnout offers an ideal complement to their time alone in their stall, and improves their overall well-being, which in turn improves their attitude under saddle.

One more word of advice for riding stallions: stallions usually have distinctive, powerful necks, the so-called "stallion neck," which is one way they typically express their masculinity. When trained correctly it is possible to encourage the stallion to stretch forward and down and carry his forehead at or slightly in front of the vertical. If the rider neglects this, she will quickly have difficulties with the position of the horse's poll and head. Although most horses will not get too deep when ridden with less than ideal contact, stallions tend to quickly react by "curling up."

Due to their pronounced crest, stallions are prone to breaking at the 3rd or 4th vertebra rather than keeping their poll as the highest point. This is often combined with head tilting—mistakes that are very negatively scored in the dressage ring. This adds to the value of stretching the neck and raising the back to avoid further problems in the horse's basics (rhythm, relaxation, contact).

With the points I've covered in mind, young stallions benefit greatly from a multidisciplinary training approach. Dressage work, jumping gymnastics, longeing, conditioning on a galloping track, trail riding, and turnout are all essential ingredients for satisfying a stallion's needs and supporting his physical and mental development.

MARES

There are widely diverging opinions when it comes to the subject of riding mares and/or competing on them. Some riders refuse to ride mares because "they are always cranky and in heat." Others swear by mares and argue that mares are more sensitive and intelligent than geldings and less complicated than stallions. The reality is probably somewhere in between. Mares do require slightly different handling and riding than their male counterparts. Hormones have a considerable effect on their nature. Some are especially "mareish," meaning they are generally very cranky and show their heat cycles very obviously, becoming complicated, moody, overly sensitive, resistant to the rider's leg aids, and disinterested in being ridden.

There are also mares whose hormonal fluctuations are barely noticeable. They are even-tempered and friendly and remain uncomplicated to ride during their heat cycle. And to further complicate things, there are some mares that are especially relaxed, friendly, and even-tempered—but only when they are in heat.

In addition to their hormone cycles, mares differ slightly from geldings and stallions in their conformation. As with humans, females and males are not built the same. Mares usually have smaller necks than stallions, more prominent bellies, often a longer loin, and are slightly straighter behind than geldings and stallions. If these conformational traits are highly pronounced, they influence the horse's movement and rideability. For example, some people use the term "mare canter" to describe how many mares seem to "scramble" along in a flatter canter than their male counterparts, due to their longer loins and straighter hind legs. Sport horse breeding has developed over the past few decades and the quality of horses has improved. The modern mare is built more athletically and is less likely to display once typical "mare qualities" such as these. And sometimes, you have to look closely to tell the difference between a mare and a gelding.

In my experience, mares that are built less like mares also act less "mareish." "Mareish" or not, mares react more sensitively than geldings and stallions. They are usually more ticklish and thus sometimes overreact to the touch of the rider's leg or spur. Perhaps mares are like human females who have twice as many receptors in the skin (cutaneous receptors) than males, making their skin much more sensitive to touch. When riding mares, this sensitivity must be taken in to account. This factor alone makes riding and training mares unique.

Common Training Mistakes

Coarsely given aids, long spurs, and nagging with the leg will make even the friendliest mare cranky, and if she is ridden like this over a significant period of time, it will have a strong negative influence on her overall rideability.

Training Tips

One often hears the saying, "When the rider succeeds in getting a mare on his side, he has a horse that will do anything for him." The question is whether this is true. It is definitely true that if ridden poorly, mares will leave their riders in a bind. Mares don't tolerate poor riding and quickly become cranky, wreaking havoc on the harmony between horse and rider, as well as on relaxation. Attentive riders with good feeling immediately notice if a mare loses her willingness to work. Mares quickly show it when something is wrong—an improperly given aid, perhaps the rider's leg was too far back or she used too much spur, usually evokes an annoyed reaction from the mare, such as pinned ears. The next level of annoyance is usually tail swishing, which can evolve to constant "tail wringing," and in extreme cases, the mare may spontaneously urinate. If the situation deteriorates this far, the horse's mental worry and annoyance has caused her muscles to become increasingly tense, which snowballs and leads to further discomfort and resistance under saddle. If the rider does not rethink her entire training method and administration of the aids at this point, very serious and long-term riding problems can occur.

The modern sport horse mare, trained in dressage with correct muscling, is difficult to discern from a gelding.

GEORGE WILLIAMS AND ROCHER

"I have been riding Rocher since 2001, and she never ceases to impress me. She is a mentally and physically capable mare with a strong sense of fairness. As her rider I have to be very careful when I correct her and make sure that I am always being fair, in return. Otherwise she will take offense, close down, and become very strong. But when she is ridden just right and feels that the aids are as they should be, she will do anything for the rider. She loves to work and to please. Luckily, she is a very even-tempered mare, even when she is in heat, which is not even noticeable when riding or handling her.

"I think mares are generally more sensitive than geldings, and are similar to stallions in a way. Stallions will also take offense at a rider or handler mistake. Unlike stallions, though, I think that most mares are more honest in the show ring. This is true for Rocher. At home she can sometimes be a challenge for the rider because of her powerful neck and strong personality. In daily work we focus on half-halts to improve her 'throughness' and to keep her on the aids. At horse shows her personality is an advantage. She is always 'on,' and seems to say, 'Hey look at me, here I come.' Rocher is a diva, but in a very positive way."

George Williams and Rocher.

Here the rider purposefully demonstrates using too much pressure with the leg and a restricting hand to "pull and push" the mare together. The mare immediately reacts by resisting. Her ears are laid back, her back is tense, and her tail swishes in annoyance.

If you know how to look, the sensitivity of a mare can actually be a good indicator of the quality of her rider's riding. For example, the mare's ears should be observed more than those of other horses. If the ears indicate annoyance or unwillingness, the rider should change her leg aids. Sometimes it is enough to use the leg in a more forward location, closer to the girth. Even an outside leg placed to prevent the haunches from falling out should not be placed too far back on a sensitive mare's side. Many mares are ticklish around their bellies toward their udder and react by freezing up or resisting.

Mares are also unlikely to accept being dominated through strength and are more likely to show their displeasure at this method than geldings. A restraining hand from the saddle, for example, will cause an especially strong negative reaction from a mare. Instead of trying to pull and force the horse with the reins, the rider should ride many half-halts, halt transitions, and rein-backs. This way the rider can attempt to persuade the mare they are partners by using more subtle and kinder aids. Then, she is more likely to cooperate.

BREED CHARACTERISTICS

Jessica Süss and Zorro.

EVERY BREED HAS ITS STRENGTHS

Breed types run the gamut, from sport to pleasure, and from English to Western. In addition, favored breeds vary from region to region, and country to country. Just as we are guilty of labeling our fellow humans via one popular stereotype or another, so we are guilty of determining how a horse will look, act, and at what activity he will excel by figuring in the prevalent characteristics of his breed.

Just some of the common stereotypes we might hear bandied about in riding rings on various continents are that Warmbloods are suitable for sport and competition, Haflingers are for trail and pleasure riding, Friesians are for carriage driving, and Andalusians are for Baroque enthusiasts. Some truth actually does lie in these stereotypes—although only a kernel. Within every breed of horse is a huge variety of different traits. And each breed has been progressively bred to serve different purposes. In recent decades, for example, Warmbloods have been selectively bred for sport purposes, whereas Haflingers have been bred to be small, surefooted horses suitable for high mountain terrain. When you consider the Friesian, the breed's origin traces back to use as carriage and parade horses—and they were selected for their high set neck and animated knee action. The fact that today the Warmblood, the Haflinger, and the Friesian all show up in dressage competitions around the world is not so much proof that these breeds are all well suited for the sport, but rather that dressage is continuously growing in popularity, even among owners of non-traditional dressage horses.

This is a perfectly acceptable development, as long as it does not negatively affect the horses involved. When purchasing a horse, the buyer must give thought to her riding goals. The ambitious, competitive-minded dressage rider should not buy herself a Friesian or a Quarter Horse. The same is true for the competitive jumper rider. These breeds are "generally" predestined for other purposes. Of course, as always, there are exceptions—but the exceptions cannot be "made," they appear by chance. For example, the owner of a talented Friesian that, in addition to knee action, has natural impulsion and elasticity, a pure three-beat canter, and a strong back, should

The Friesian's naturally high-set neck looks very impressive, but can lead to problems under saddle.

SPOTLIGHT: FRIESIANS

Breed-Specific Muscular Issues

"Riders often correctly sense that different breeds have muscular differences, and therefore, varying muscular problems. In the field of equine physical therapy, many such differences are commonly recognized. For example, most Friesians with their naturally high-set neck have very pronounced neck muscling. When a physical therapist focuses on working with these neck muscles, it becomes apparent that the brachiocephalic muscle and the muscles on the sides of the neck are often quite 'hard,' which makes bending left and right, flexion, and even balance, difficult for the horse. Physical therapy that is intended to raise the horse's back, and especially his withers, is generally more difficult for Friesians, and the desired lift sometimes occurs three to four vertebrae back from the ideal. It can be said that, on average, Friesians have shorter, and therefore, stiffer backs than Warmbloods, although back problems are unfortunately very common in Warmbloods, as well.

certainly try to further the horse's dressage training, if that is in her interests. But if your lovely Friesian lacks these qualities, forcing the issue will only be to your frustration and possible detriment to your horse's health.

A rider that has her heart set on riding upper-level dressage and chooses a Friesian because she is enthralled by his looks—after all, he is a beautiful and impressive black horse—runs the risk of eventually overtaxing, and therefore, unfairly treating the horse. This scenario is true for all breeds that are bred for a specific purpose other than that which their owners, who are enchanted by their appearance, color, or temperament, have planned for them.

This is not to say that owners of certain horse breeds should only ride on trails or in breed demonstrations. Basic dressage training is, in fact, important and healthy for every horse. And, in this process the exceptionally talented members of the breed that defy the

"Many Friesian riders ride their horse in a too high frame, meaning that the long back muscle, the *longissimus dorsi*, barely stretches. The horse can only raise his back as we'd like when the back muscles stretch. In relation to this, many Friesians lack developed stomach muscles. The stomach muscles are best strengthened by riding long and low.

"Due to the Friesians unique movement, problems often occur in their chest muscles, which raise and lower their front legs and can become hardened and tight. This problem also occurs in Quarter Horses, although they have completely different conformation than Friesians. In the case of the Quarter Horse, the horse's weight rests on the forehand, causing a considerable burden and inherent stress.

"Other horses experience muscle imbalances, although often this occurs less due to their conformation and more due to the way they are ridden. Every time a muscle is tensed it must be relaxed again. When this balance of tension and relaxation doesn't occur, painful results can follow." (For more on Friesians, see p. 149.)

—*Martina Rosenhagen, Certified Equine Physical Therapist*

stereotypes can be discovered. Nonetheless these achievements are reserved for the exceptions and usually do not represent the breeding goals of the respective registries. If all horses were bred to excel in the dressage arena, the charm and individuality of each breed would disappear until they could eventually only be differentiated by their papers.

On the pages that follow, I discuss several vastly different breeds that it is not so unusual to see in the dressage ring today. This is meant to serve only as a sample comparison; including the other approximately 300 or so breeds is clearly beyond the scope of this book.

WARMBLOODS

Categorizing horses as "Warmbloods" is really a very vague description, since every horse that is not a "cold blood," Thoroughbred, Standardbred, Arabian, or pony can likely be considered one. When I speak of Warmbloods I mean the sport horses originally bred in Germany, the Netherlands, France, Denmark, and Sweden. These horses were selectively bred for generations to be capable dressage and jumping horses. Breed standards do not differ greatly between the various Warmblood registries, so you must often look at the horse's brand in order to determine the country in which he was bred and the registry to which he belongs.

The modern Warmblood sport horse is typically a medium-to-large horse (15.3 to 17.3hh) with a rectangular build; elastic movement; harmonious proportions; an elegant head that fits the size of the body; and a well-set and slightly rounded neck of medium length that emerges from a well-defined—neither too high nor too flat—wither. The shoulder should be long and sloping, and the torso should include a wide chest and deep girth to allow plenty of space for the lungs and heart. The back should have a slightly concave outline, be neither too short nor too long, and end at a slightly rounded croup.

Common Training Mistakes

It is neither correct to lump all Warmbloods together nor to philosophize about vast differences between the different registries. With a few exceptions (i.e., Holsteiner, Trakehner) the Warmblood registries have "open books," meaning that horses can be crossed with other breeds. This means there are horses branded by one registry that have ancestors from all different registries in their pedigree. It is, therefore, just as incorrect to presume that Hanoverians have certain characteristics, whereas Westfalians have other characteristics, as it is to generalize that all Warmbloods are "difficult." Each horse must be considered as an individual with unique qualities and temperament.

Training Tips

There is an old saying, "You don't ride the pedigree," which is generally true. If a horse is talented and has good rideability, it is of little importance whether well known or unknown ancestors are listed in his papers (if he has them). Nevertheless, there are certain bloodlines that, over generations, have become known for producing especially willing or especially difficult horses. When choosing a horse,

Warmbloods have been selectively bred as sport horses for generations. A common breed ideal is for the horse to exhibit big, swinging gaits.

the buyer should definitely be aware as to which such characteristics are known to be passed down by the line in question. This way the buyer, especially of a young horse, can hopefully avoid purchasing a horse that is unsuitable for the intended purpose.

There are also bloodlines known for certain physical characteristics. For example, horses from some lines take longer to mature and finish growing, whereas other lines are known to produce horses with slightly weak backs. In these cases it is important for the rider to be informed of tendencies toward these traits so that she can appropriately adjust her riding, while still following the Training Scale (see p. 17).

HAFLINGERS

The blond to light chestnut ponies (usually 13.2 to 14.2hh) with a light mane and tail are equipped with a powerful neck, stout body, muscular hindquarters, and short, strong legs. The breed emerged in Austria in the 1800s. In the following decades the small horses became popular in mountainous areas where they were used by

When a Haflinger is correctly gymnasticized, he can be a capable and pleasant dressage horse.

farmers and forest workers. Today Haflingers are popular trail and pleasure horses, especially in parts of Europe, due to their surefootedness and friendly natures. They are also used in a variety of other sports, including driving, Western riding, and dressage.

Even though this Haflinger will never be shown at Grand Prix level, the benefit of half-steps can be seen in the picture on the right, as he steps much further under his body with his hind legs.

Common Training Mistakes
As with all horses, especially those of small stature and specific body type, it is a mistake to try to make a Haflinger into something that he is not. At the same time, it is also a mistake to forgo his basic training in dressage, which can improve his health and athleticism.

Training Tips
It is safe to say Haflingers aren't known for their potential as top dressage horses. Even though there are a few individuals that have mastered Grand Prix movements, most Haflingers that compete in dressage appear in Training and First Level, and sometimes even Second Level tests. Generally speaking, they do not have the quality of gaits that is a prerequisite for riding at the higher levels. Nonetheless, training this breed in basic dressage in accordance with the Training Scale (see p. 17) will improve the horse's rideability, put him on the aids, and help to preserve the horse's health.

Since most Haflingers are equipped with a "ground-bound" and somewhat heavy-footed trot and canter, their training should focus on an optimal contact, active hind legs that step under the body, improved "throughness," and overall correctness of the dressage movements. While the majority of Haflingers cannot be trained to have a jaw-dropping, show-stopping trot, they can become very reliable partners for the lower level dressage rider. (As is always the case, it is not out of the question for an exceptionally talented horse-and-rider pair to go further.)

The breed's usually short, powerful neck and short, wide back require special attention. A clever rider can succeed in "pulling" the neck into an apparent frame, but as with all horses, this will negatively affect the elasticity of the back, as well as suppleness and relaxation in general. It helps to work these horses long and low—improving their willingness and ability to stretch forward and down should be a priority. This not only lifts the back, but also the withers, which positively influences the quality of the horse's gaits. As the withers lift, the horse moves with a freer shoulder, and therefore, a freer foreleg. In this way, the somewhat "stomping" gait of the Haflinger can become lighter and more expressive.

The Haflinger's back is adept at carrying loads but is somewhat limited in its sideways movement. Since Haflingers were originally bred as pack horses in the mountains, half-passes were not in their job description! The flexibility of the back can be improved through movements such as shoulder-in, travers (haunches-in), renvers (haunches-out), and half-pass, which also increase the "carrying" and "pushing power" of the hind legs and promote impulsion. Due to the horse's build, the rider should neither expect nor force a Haflinger to perform exaggerated sideways steps or movements.

As mentioned earlier, the canter can be a difficult for the Haflinger used as a dressage horse. It tends to be short-strided, flat, and somewhat hurried. Once the horse's general suppleness is improved the canter can begin to take shape. Within limits, in-hand work can be helpful. The goal in this case is not to teach a Haflinger to piaffe, but rather to use half-steps to quicken the horse's hind legs and increase the carrying capacity of the hind end. Over time this will have a positive effect on the horse's movement.

A rider that chooses a Haflinger as his mount chooses an equine partner rather than a high level dressage or jumping career. He is usually getting a horse with an uncomplicated character, and a versatile pleasure horse that can also compete at low levels successfully.

The Haflinger's somewhat problematic canter can be improved through dressage work to increase the carrying capacity of the hind legs. It is important that the horse learn not to rely on the rider's hand for balance.

FRIESIANS

In recent years, Friesians have gained an impressive following. The story of these so-called "Black Pearls" traces back to the sixteenth and seventeenth centuries, when draft horses used for farming and pulling carriages in West Friesland (a province of the Netherlands) were supposedly crossed with the Andalusian war horses belonging to Spanish troops. The resulting cross was primarily used for agrarian pulling power, but was also considered a fine riding and carriage horse. By the beginning of the twentieth century the breed had almost disappeared, but it has since experienced a renaissance.

The modern Friesian is an imposing black horse standing 15.2 to 16.3hh, with a high-set neck, round, powerful hindquarters, a luxurious mane and tail, feathered legs, and a pronounced knee action in the trot. The breed is used both as a riding and driving horse, for both pleasure and competition.

The long-haired "dream horse" of many modern riders: the Friesian.

A A powerful Friesian stallion with conformation typical of the breed, including a massive, high-set neck and a slightly concave back.

B A stallion of the same age but of a slightly lighter type. The neck is carried somewhat lower and the back is a little less concave.

Common Training Mistakes

It is ignorant to believe that just because of their beauty and style Friesians are suitable dressage horses. The Friesian's particular conformation and unique movement bring with them many problems when applied to the sport. As with other breeds, however, it is also wrong to completely ignore basic dressage training as it can be of great benefit to the horse, regardless of his "job" or "purpose."

Training Tips

A rider who has ambitious plans for her dressage career with her sights set on competing at the upper levels or even internationally, should probably not choose a Friesian as her dressage partner. Unless, of course, she happens to come across an exceptionally talented Friesian with a swinging, light-footed trot and canter, a strong back, and healthy joints (I talk more about these points in the pages that follow).

Most Friesians have impressive knee action but are equipped with somewhat "stamping," heavy-footed gaits. This is combined with the naturally high-set and (usually) massive neck, which, unfortunately, Friesian enthusiasts commonly confuse with self-carriage. As we've touched on, the latter occurs only through the raising of the horse's back and simultaneous lowering of his hindquarters as they increase their carrying capacity. If the rider accepts the high head carriage of

A You can clearly see how during the simple cavalletti exercise this young Friesian finds it difficult to let his neck reach forward and downward.

B Despite the difficulties associated with their breed type, a few exceptionally talented and correctly trained Friesians have made it to the higher levels of dressage competition.

the Friesian and neglects to ride the horse long and low, problems will occur, especially with contact (and this is a particular problem when starting a young horse). In addition, many Friesian-lovers choose to ride stallions, which have even bigger necks, and so they will experience a magnified version of this problem (see further discussion of the issue of training stallions on p. 126).

Many Friesians with naturally good gaits as young horses "lose" their talent over time because their rider focuses more on creating a spectacular show than on confirming the Training Scale. It is true that working through the basic elements of the Training Scale is not particularly exciting, but it creates sustained results. Friesians are an example of an instance when the rider must work on contact before the element of rhythm. Without a correct connection, which can only be reached by stretching the horse long and low, Friesians tend to have rhythm mistakes, especially in canter.

Unfortunately, when you look around today's riding stables, dressage rings, and show arenas, you will see many examples of Friesians with flawed training: The horses are frequently much too short in the neck; behind the vertical with their neck bent at the wrong vertebrae; have a dropped back; trail their hind legs behind; and exhibit heavy-footed "stamping" or spastic "flailing" of the legs in trot and lumbering four-beat canters.

For these reasons, and others, Friesians now have a poor reputation in the eyes of many dressage judges. But Friesians don't have to be this way. When correctly trained in accordance with the Training Scale, many Friesians can be successful at Second and Third Level dressage, and there are a number of talented individuals that have made it all the way to Grand Prix, such as Jorrit and Tinus under US-based Sabine Schut-Kery, or Adel 357 under Belgian Marc-Peter Spahn. However, these are unusually exceptional horses under optimal training conditions.

So, how does one train a Friesian optimally? For one thing, Friesians are generally late developers and should not be started under saddle before age four. Even then patience is required as Friesians are often one to two years behind other sport horses in their maturation process.

Due to Friesians unique conformation, they have a very shallow depth of girth and therefore have lungs up to a third smaller than

Two Friesian stallions of the same age. The horse on the left is stretching in the long and low position (although his nose could ideally reach more forward) and his left hind leg is stepping nicely under his body. The horse on the right exhibits a high neck position with trailing hind legs—note how his hindquarters have not lowered, despite the raising of his neck. The yellow circle shows that the horse on the left has raised his back and so the rider sits in the middle of the circle. The red circle on the right highlights how the horse's back is dropped and there is more "horse" behind the rider than in front of her—the horse is out of balance.

other horses of equal weight. Thus, it is advisable to use interval training with these horses, switching frequently between work and breaks. This prevents the horse's breaths per minute (bpm) from becoming too elevated as well as muscle fatigue.

To remedy the problems associated with the Friesian's high neck, the rider should focus on stretching the horse long and low. "Low" alone is not enough because these horses tend to lower their neck but curl it in toward their body. When the horse curls up behind the vertical, the rider can neither maintain a correct connection nor

Highest Point

Poll

Keeping the poll the highest point is not easy for Friesian stallions or their rider.

A Stretching forward and down is especially important for Friesians.

B When long-and-low work is combined with appropriate gymnasticizing, such as half-steps (shown here), the horse's hind legs can be brought more under his center of gravity. It is crucial not to push the horse too hard or too fast during this process.

raise the horse's back. Instead the problem with the high-set neck is only magnified, and other issues, such as the horse "breaking" at the wrong vertebrae (see p. 114) can follow. The best way to encourage the horse to reach forward with his nose is through trot work over poles and cavalletti. In addition, riding bending lines while leg-yielding and asking for haunches-out—so that the hind legs cross, ideally on the "open" side of the circle—is helpful for getting the horse's neck to relax and reach forward, provided the rider uses enough inside leg to outside rein and allows the stretch to occur.

Frequent transitions between the gaits, especially between trot and walk, help teach the horse to accept the half-halt. During downward transitions the rider must be sure to immediately drive the horse energetically forward into the contact before he has the chance to shorten or curl his neck. With this in mind, riding halt transitions from trot or canter is not an ideal exercise for Friesians, at least not until the contact is much improved.

Friesians are capable of compressing their neck like an accordion, so much so that the throatlatch and chin almost touch the neck. In the moment when this occurs it is impossible to maintain correct contact, and the horse's back will drop and the hind legs will trail out behind. Trailing hind legs are the second-biggest problem seen

The Friesian benefits when you take the time to build his trust through praise and calm handling.

in Friesians. The pressure this movement fault places on the horse's sacroiliac joint induces the horse to further unload his hind legs by simply trailing his legs further behind and raising his neck to maintain balance. Thus, the problem is compounded.

To take the problem a step further, the incorrect angle of the horse's pelvis and hind legs has a negative effect on the ligaments in the stifle, possibly overstretching them and leading to eventual upward fixation of the patella. Over time, arthritis of the joint can occur. For this reason alone it is extremely important to stretch the Friesian's neck, raise his back, and increase the ability of the hind legs to step forward under his body.

It is not only for health reasons that focus should be directed at strengthening the back and activating the hind legs. Horses that tend to drop their back, raise their neck, and trail their hind legs behind eventually lose their desire to go forward. You often see Friesians that barely move forward, are difficult for their rider to sit, or are considered lazy (see p. 56). Once a Friesian is "behind the leg," the rider must completely change her approach to correct the problem. With patience and a little luck, she can reverse the scenario and encourage the horse to once again move freely forward.

ANDALUSIANS OR PRE (PURE SPANISH HORSES)

Every Iberian-type horse bred in Spain that is not a cold blood or pony is called an Andalusian. When the horse is registered under their strict guidelines, he is then called a *Pura Rasa Española* or PRE to signify a horse of pure Spanish breeding.

The result of work in accordance with the Training Scale is an improved connection in trot and canter and a horse that carries his head in front of the vertical.

GÜNTHER FRÖHLICH AND FRIESIANS FOR DRESSAGE

"These days one sees more and more Friesians with nice conformation, good movement, and hind legs that step well under the horse's body. But there are also many Friesians that are, and should remain, simply pleasure horses. A horse's basic characteristics cannot be changed. A rider that wants a Friesian to compete in dressage must search for one with the necessary qualities. Some Friesians can be just as successful in dressage as a Warmblood.

Günther Fröhlich and one of his Friesians.

"Riders should be aware that Friesians differ slightly in their conformation and temperaments from other breeds. Friesians are very loving and interested in people, but they don't take well to being pushed and pulled around, as the Iberian breeds do, for example. Friesians can quickly take offense, close themselves off, and become stubborn. Due to their unique respiratory rate, pulse, and temperature, they must be worked a little differently and cannot be 'powered up' quite as much as other horses. Your biggest challenge is to take a quiet horse and make something dynamic out of him. You must 'kindle his fire' by offering variety in his work and allowing him time to develop. Once a Friesian 'ignites,' he is simply wonderful."

Andalusians, to use the conventional term, are square in build with medium-to-short conformational lines and a minimum height of approximately 15hh for stallions and 14.3hh for mares. They have wide, well-muscled, and relatively high-set necks, a well-muscled back with short, wide loins, and a wide, muscled croup.

This breed has a reputation for being intelligent and friendly and enjoy widespread popularity in Baroque horse circles. Because of their steady temperaments, willingness to learn, their luxurious,

The noble Andalusian—when registered, he is called a PRE (Pure Spanish Horse).

Despite difficulties due to their short stature, PRE horses have gained a foothold in international dressage competition.

wavy manes and tails, and frequently dramatic white coats they are in high demand as "show" horses—for liberty and breed demonstrations, or in combination with stunts and acrobatics on the "equine spectacular" stage. Their success in the dressage ring is limited as their short stature, which is a desired characteristic of the breed, often leads to a lack of freedom in the gaits and ground-cover at the walk, a trot that lacks "swing," and a canter that—because of its high knee action—has a four-beat tendency.

Common Training Mistakes
Even though Andalusians tend to be uncomplicated and friendly, you can't forget that every horse is different, every horse is unique. This

breed cannot simply be put on "auto pilot," especially when it comes to pursuing a competitive dressage career with one as your partner.

Some Spanish horses have large, ground covering trots, but they remain the exception. Even in this impressive demonstration, the horse's nose should come more in front of the vertical to allow for additional lengthening of his frame and stride.

Training Tips

The Spanish dressage team has a record of impressive performances and medals to prove that Andalusians can excel on an international level. Nonetheless, the average amateur rider who enjoys competing at the lower levels in small- to medium-sized local shows should not expect too much more from her Spanish-bred mount. Although her horse may be very beautiful and appear to have much talent for collected work, it is a long and difficult path to the upper levels (when canter pirouettes, piaffe, and passage are required, the Andalusian can bring his strengths to the table). Quality of the gaits is considered as well as collection as you advance through the lower levels. And, the Andalusian's gaits generally look different than those of the Warmblood, for example. The short, wide back that is highly desirable in these Baroque horses (longer lines are considered a fault in this breed), as well as the upright pasterns that allow for high, lavish knee action, usually have a negative effect on elasticity of the gaits.

Since the Andalusian's short back characterizes and also limits the quality of his movement, he should be worked according to the guidelines laid out in the section on the short-coupled horse (see p. 84). This means riding and longeing over trot poles and cavalletti; increased riding of bending lines, including voltes and serpen-

JEAN BEMELMANS AND SPANISH HORSES FOR DRESSAGE

"Before I began working with Spanish horses, I primarily had experience with Warmbloods. In the end, regardless of whether a horse is of Baroque-type or Warmblood build, he needs good, basic dressage training that can be used as a foundation and that a rider can turn back to when and if problems arise. Nonetheless there are specific areas that are more difficult for Spanish horses due to their conformation, and these must receive special attention while training.

"Andalusians are very short, compact horses that tend to lack 'swing' through the back. If the rider doesn't stretch this type of horse long and low, eventually *nothing* will work properly. When I first started working with the Spanish dressage team, many riders tended to work their horse in absolute elevation, believing that this enhanced their appearance. However, it only caused their horse to be tight in the back and to demonstrate hurried movement, since the movement could not be generated from the 'engine' of the hind legs and propelled forward over a 'swinging' back.

tines; lateral movements of all kinds, including shoulder-in, travers (haunches-in), and renvers (haunches-out); and letting the horse canter outside the confines of the arena, on a galloping track if possible. In summary, the Spanish horse must be convinced to let his strong and high-set neck relax and reach down from the withers, stretching into a steady contact with the rider's hand (in which some pressure on the bit initiated by the horse is appropriate) in order to stretch the back muscles. This way the naturally highly elevated gaits of the horse can increase their forward reach and the steps and strides can be lengthened in all three gaits.

"To correct this, the horses had to be worked in a relative elevation rather than absolute elevation. This included returning to the long-and-low stretching position. During warm-up, the team rode with a somewhat deeper neck carriage and rode half-halts within the gaits to improve the horse's rhythm and cadence. Allowing the gaits to swing while maintaining their rhythm enables the impulsion generated in the hind legs to travel over the back to the bit, thereby making stretching possible.

"Many Spanish horses tend to 'trot like a pony' when in the stretching position, but ultimately, this doesn't matter. I have a gelding that does this, but then after the stretching phase, once his back is supple and 'swings' and he can legitimately assume a higher head carriage, he trots very well—almost like a Warmblood!

"In addition to increased stretching work, I work these horses more intensely in lateral movements. Shoulder-in, travers (haunches-in), renvers (haunches-out), shallow and steep half-passes all improve the 'throughness' and suppleness more than if the horse only traveled straight ahead. Correct bending work is good for all horses, but especially for Andalusians. When they are only ridden on straight lines, then tension occurs."

Jean Bemelmans